HOMI K. BHABHA

Homi K. Bhabha is one of the most important figures in contemporary post-colonial studies. This volume explores Bhabha's writings and their influence on post-colonial theory, clearly introducing key concepts developed in his work, such as:

- the stereotype
- mimicry
- hybridity
- the uncanny
- the nation
- cultural rights

David Huddart draws examples from a range of fields including cultural theory, film and literary studies in order to illustrate the practical application of Bhabha's thought. Offering a starting point for readers new to this crucial theorist's sometimes complex texts, or support for those who wish to deepen their understanding of his work, this guidebook is ideal for students in the fields of literary, cultural and post-colonial theory.

David Huddart is Assistant Professor of English Literature at the Chinese Universtiy of Hong Kong.

ROUTLEDGE CRITICAL THINKERS

Series Editor: Robert Eaglestone, Royal Holloway, University of London

Routledge Critical Thinkers is a series of accessible introductions to key figures in contemporary critical thought.

With a unique focus on historical and intellectual contexts, each volume examines a key theorist's:

- significance
- motivation
- key ideas and their sources
- impact on other thinkers

Concluding with extensively annotated guides to further reading, *Routledge Critical Thinkers* are the student's passport to today's most exciting critical thought.

Already available:

For further details on this series, see http://www.routledge.com/literature

HOMI K. BHABHA

David Huddart

 Routledge
Taylor & Francis Group

LONDON AND NEW YORK

First published 2006
by Routledge
2 Park Square, Milton Park, Abingdon, Oxon OX14 4RN

Simultaneously published in the USA and Canada
by Routledge
270 Madison Ave, New York, NY 10016

Routledge is an imprint of the Taylor & Francis Group

Transferred to Digital Printing 2006

© 2006 David Huddart

Typeset in Perpetua by Taylor & Francis

British Library Cataloguing in Publication Data
A catalogue record for this book is available from the British Library

Library of Congress Cataloging-in-Publication Data
A catalog record for this book has been requested

ISBN 0-415-32823-3 (hbk)
ISBN 0-415-32824-1 (pbk)

ISBN 13 978-0-415-32823-4 (hbk)
ISBN 13 978-0-415-32824-1 (pbk)

Publisher's Note
The publisher has gone to great lengths to ensure the quality
of this reprint but points out that some imperfections
in the original may be apparent

T&F informa
Taylor & Francis Group is the Academic Division of T&F Informa plc.

CONTENTS

SERIES EDITOR'S PREFACE

The books in this series offer introductions to major critical thinkers who have influenced literary studies and the humanities. The *Routledge Critical Thinkers* series provides the books you can turn to first when a new name or concept appears in your studies.

Each book will equip you to approach a key thinker's original texts by explaining her or his key ideas, putting them into context and, perhaps most importantly, showing you why this thinker is considered to be significant. The emphasis is on concise, clearly written guides which do not presuppose a specialist knowledge. Although the focus is on particular figures, the series stresses that no critical thinker ever existed in a vacuum but, instead, emerged from a broader intellectual, cultural and social history. Finally, these books will act as a bridge between you and the thinker's original texts: not replacing them but rather complementing what she or he wrote.

These books are necessary for a number of reasons. In his 1997 autobiography, *Not Entitled*, the literary critic Frank Kermode wrote of a time in the 1960s:

> On beautiful summer lawns, young people lay together all night, recovering from their daytime exertions and listening to a troupe of Balinese musicians. Under their blankets or their sleeping bags, they would chat drowsily about the gurus of the time.... What they repeated was largely hearsay; hence my

lunchtime suggestion, quite impromptu, for a series of short, very cheap
books offering authoritative but intelligible introductions to such figures.

There is still a need for 'authoritative and intelligible introductions'. But this series reflects a different world from the 1960s. New
thinkers have emerged and the reputations of others have risen and
fallen, as new research has developed. New methodologies and challenging ideas have spread through the arts and humanities. The study
of literature is no longer – if it ever was – simply the study and evalu-
ation of poems, novels, and plays. It is also the study of the ideas,
issues, and difficulties which arise in any literary text and in its interpretation. Other arts and humanities subjects have changed in analogous ways.

With these changes, new problems have emerged. The ideas and
issues behind these radical changes in the humanities are often presented without reference to wider contexts or as theories which you
can simply 'add on' to the texts you read. Certainly, there's nothing
wrong with picking out selected ideas or using what comes to hand –
indeed, some thinkers have argued that this is, in fact, all we can do.
However, it is sometimes forgotten that each new idea comes from the
pattern and development of somebody's thought and it is important to
study the range and context of their ideas. Against theories 'floating in
space', the *Routledge Critical Thinkers* series places key thinkers and
their ideas firmly back in their contexts.

More than this, these books reflect the need to go back to the
thinker's own texts and ideas. Every interpretation of an idea, even the
most seemingly innocent one, offers its own 'spin', implicitly or explicitly. To read only books on a thinker, rather than texts by that thinker, is
to deny yourself a chance of making up your own mind. Sometimes
what makes a significant figure's work hard to approach is not so much
its style or content as the feeling of not knowing where to start. The
purpose of these books is to give you a 'way in' by offering an accessible
overview of these thinkers' ideas and works and by guiding your further reading, starting with each thinker's own texts. To use a metaphor
from the philosopher Ludwig Wittgenstein (1889–1951), these books
are ladders, to be thrown away after you have climbed to the next level.
Not only, then, do they equip you to approach new ideas, but also they

empower you, by leading you back to a theorist's own texts and encouraging you to develop your own informed opinions.

Finally, these books are necessary because, just as intellectual needs have changed, the education systems around the world – the contexts in which introductory books are usually read – have changed radically, too. What was suitable for the minority higher education system of the 1960s is not suitable for the larger, wider, more diverse, high technology education systems of the twenty-first century. These changes call not just for new, up-to-date introductions but new methods of presentation. The presentational aspects of *Routledge Critical Thinkers* have been developed with today's students in mind.

Each book in the series has a similar structure. They begin with a section offering an overview of the life and ideas of each thinker and explain why she or he is important. The central section of each book discusses the thinker's key ideas, their context, evolution and reception. Each book concludes with a survey of the thinker's impact, outlining how their ideas have been taken up and developed by others. In addition, there is a detailed final section suggesting and describing books for further reading. This is not a 'tacked-on' section but an integral part of each volume. In the first part of this section you will find brief descriptions of the thinker's key works, then, following this, information on the most useful critical works and, in some cases, on relevant websites. This section will guide you in your reading, enabling you to follow your interests and develop your own projects. Throughout each book, references are given in what is known as the Harvard system (the author and the date of a work cited are given in the text and you can look up the full details in the bibliography at the back). This offers a lot of information in very little space. The books also explain technical terms and use boxes to describe events or ideas in more detail, away from the main emphasis of the discussion. Boxes are also used at times to highlight definitions of terms frequently used or coined by a thinker. In this way, the boxes serve as a kind of glossary, easily identified when flicking through the book.

The thinkers in the series are 'critical' for three reasons. First, they are examined in the light of subjects which involve criticism: principally literary studies or English and cultural studies, but also other disciplines which rely on the criticism of books, ideas, theories and unquestioned assumptions. Second, they are critical because studying their work will provide you with a 'tool kit' for your own informed critical reading and thought, which will make you critical. Third, these thinkers are critical because they are crucially important: they deal with ideas and questions which can overturn conventional understandings of the world, of texts, of everything we take for granted, leaving us with a deeper understanding of what we already knew and with new ideas.

No introduction can tell you everything. However, by offering a way into critical thinking, this series hopes to begin to engage you in an activity which is productive, constructive and potentially life-changing.

ACKNOWLEDGEMENTS

I would like to thank Liz Thompson and Robert Eaglestone for their assistance and suggestions during the writing of this book. I would also like to thank Mark Jerng and Homi Bhabha for practical assistance. Finally, for various kinds of support, I would like to thank David Coughlan, David Ewick, Bart Moore-Gilbert, Makiko Niederstrasser, James Quan-Nicholls, Masaki Tomochi, Huiwen Shi and Bernard Wilson.

ABBREVIATIONS

References to interviews, articles, and books by Homi Bhabha are abbreviated in the text as follows. Publication details for these and other works by Bhabha are in the 'Further Reading' section. For references to texts by other authors, full details are found in 'Works cited'.

AN	'Anxious Nations, Nervous States' (1994)
ANI	'Art and National Identity' (1991)
ATL	'At the Limits' (1989)
BM	'"Black Male": The Whitney Museum of American Art' (1995)
CM	'Cosmopolitanisms' (2000)
CSP	'Caliban Speaks to Prospero' (1991)
DBD	'Day by Day … With Frantz Fanon' (1996)
DC	'Designer Creations' (1997)
DD	'Democracy De-realized' (2003)
DV	'Double Visions' (1992)
HH	'Halfway House' (1997)
JA	'Joking Aside: the Idea of a Self-critical Community' (1998)
LC	*The Location of Culture* (1994)
LSC	'Liberalism's Sacred Cow' (1997)
MD	'Making Difference' (2003)
NN	'Narrating the Nation' in *Nation and Narration* (1991)
OM	'On Minorities: Cultural Rights' (2000)
OQ	'The Other Question' (1983)
PA	'Postcolonial Authority and Postmodern Guilt' (1992)

RB   'Re-Inventing Britain: A Manifesto' (1997)
ST   'Surviving Theory' (2000)
TP   'Threatening Pleasures' (1991)
TS   'Third Space' (1991)
TT   'Translator Translated' (1995)
WH   'The World and the Home' (1992)
WR   'On Writing Rights' (2003)
WS   'The White Stuff' (1998)

1
WHY BHABHA?

Homi K. Bhabha was born in 1949 in Mumbai, India. He is one of the most important thinkers in the influential movement in cultural theory called post-colonial criticism. Bhabha's work develops a set of challenging concepts that are central to post-colonial theory: hybridity, mimicry, difference, ambivalence. These concepts describe ways in which colonized peoples have resisted the power of the colonizer, a power that is never as secure as it seems to be. This emphasis illuminates our present situation, in a world marked by a paradoxical combination of violently proclaimed cultural difference and the complexly interconnected networks of globalization. Instead of seeing colonialism as something locked in the past, Bhabha shows how its histories and cultures constantly intrude on the present, demanding that we transform our understanding of cross-cultural relations. The authority of dominant nations and ideas is never as complete as it seems, because it is always marked by anxiety, something that enables the dominated to fight back.

To demonstrate this anxiety, Bhabha looks back to the histories of colonialism. In 1914, almost 85% of the world's land surface was under the control of a small group of mainly European colonial powers. Yet the consequence of this control was not simple domination.

We should not see the colonial situation as one of straightforward oppression of the colonized by the colonizer. Alongside violence and domination, we might also see the last five hundred years as a period of complex and varied cultural contact and interaction. In fact, the colonial period is ongoing, and post-colonial perspectives contribute an original understanding of our colonial present. Bhabha's work is a main driver behind the creation of such post-colonial perspectives. His writings bring resources from literary and cultural theory to the study of, in the first instance, a colonial archive that seems to be a simple expression of the colonizer's domination of the colonized. Bhabha's close textual analysis finds the hidden gaps and anxieties present in the colonial situation. These points of textual anxiety mark moments in which the colonizer was less powerful than was apparent, moments when the colonized were able to resist the dominance exercised over them. In short, Bhabha's work emphasizes the active *agency* of the colonized.

Of course the study of colonialism has always focused on certain kinds of colonial agency, particularly violent anti-colonial struggle. Decolonization did not just quietly happen, but had to be forced by colonized people rebelling against colonial authority. However, the agency studied by Bhabha is not the same as this revolutionary agency. His work is original because it does two connected things. First, it provides a conceptual vocabulary for the reading of colonial and post-colonial texts, beginning with those of British India in the nineteenth century. As I have outlined, this reading shows how rigid distinctions between the colonizer and colonized have always been impossible to maintain. Second, through its conceptual vocabulary Bhabha's work demonstrates that the West is troubled by its 'doubles', in particular the East. These doubles force the West to explain its own identity and to justify its rational self-image. Western civilization is not unique, nor simply Western, and its 'superiority' is not something that can be confidently asserted when other civilizations are so similar. So, on the one hand, Bhabha examines colonial history; on the other, he rethinks the present moment, when colonialism seems a thing of the past.

These two aspects of his work are connected. Colonial doubling is something that troubles the self-image of the colonizer; similarly, the

East troubles the bounded self-image of the West. Such doubling is something Bhabha finds throughout colonial and post-colonial texts, particularly literary texts with their frequent forays into the fantastic, the monstrous, and the uncanny. Because literature is so often a matter of doubling, it is for Bhabha central to the processes of his post-colonial perspective, a perspective that re-imagines the West and reminds it of its repressed colonial origins. But it is not only literature, more language in general that inspires Bhabha's methods, particularly the idea that language is not a straightforward communication of meaning. This is important because the meaning of culture is not simply imposed by the colonizer. The colonizer's cultural meanings are open to transformation by the colonized population: like any text, the meaning of colonial text cannot be controlled by its authors. When colonizer and colonized come together, there is an element of *negotiation* of cultural meaning. Bhabha's work explores how language transforms the way identities are structured when colonizer and colonized interact, finding that colonialism is marked by a complex economy of identity in which colonized and colonizer depend on each other. As I have said, his work stresses and extends the agency of colonized peoples, whose participation in resistance to colonialism has often been underplayed when it does not fit our usual expectations of violent anti-colonial opposition: importantly, he develops a *linguistic* model of this agency.

Although many of his most influential writings were originally published during the 1980s, Bhabha is very much a thinker for the twenty-first century. The complex doublings he finds in the colonial archive have continued relevance. In the years following 9/11 (the destruction by terrorists of New York's World Trade Center in September 2001), this relevance has become more obvious. Recently Bhabha's work has begun to explore the complexities of a world marked by colonial and neo-colonial wars, counter-globalization movements and widespread cultural confrontation. We are faced with a world seemingly polarized and divided into discrete cultures. This situation is often described, in the words of historian Bernard Lewis, as a 'clash of civilizations' (2004). This description sees differences as being cultural rather than political: this usually means that historical events are explained as arising from innate cultural differences, implying that we cannot reconcile oppositions (e.g. oppositions between Islam and the West, or 'Jihad vs McWorld'). Bhabha shows how such polarization is simplistic and dangerous, as it ignores the continuing processes of history. In particular, Bhabha explores how colonialism is still very much with us. Colonialism conditions the world in which we live in complex ways. But we cannot explain this by dividing the world into the good (the formerly oppressed) and the bad (the former oppressors). Bhabha's writings complicate what we think we know about colonialism and its legacies. Accordingly, Bhabha's rewritten perspectives on colonialism demand a more complex understanding of the present moment, which is never quite as radically new as it seems.

METHODS: COLONIAL DISCOURSE ANALYSIS

The methods behind Bhabha's perspective are significant. His work transformed the study of colonialism by applying post-structuralist methodologies to colonial texts. *Post-structuralism* refers to the work of many distinct writers, whose work is not always connected in any explicit way: it usually refers to the work of philosophers like Gilles Deleuze (1925–1995), Michel Foucault (1926–1984) and Jacques Derrida (1930–2004). If this work could be reduced to a single explanatory term, that term would be *difference*. For example, even in writing, post-structuralists find differences and complexities that mean texts do not say what they initially seem to say, what they want to say, or what we think they say. Likewise, in our own sense of ourselves – our identity or subjectivity – these thinkers find division and difference. Such insights can be extended beyond philosophical issues to broad historical and cultural contexts. Cultural difference is often an implicit theme, and is sometimes explicitly discussed. And Bhabha explores and extends this relevance of post-structuralism for cultural difference.

Bhabha's work takes post-structuralist approaches and applies them to colonialism, producing what has been called 'colonial discourse analysis'. For most of the twentieth century, the study of colonialism was dominated by Marxist perspectives – understandable, given that

Marxism had an important role in the traditions of anti-colonialism. Perhaps the most significant challenge to this emphasis was that of Edward W. Said (1935–2003). Said's most influential work has been *Orientalism* (1978), a study of the coherence of Western discourses about 'the Orient' or the East. Said argues that the way people in the West discussed the Orient developed a set of discourses of orientalism which set up an allegedly superior Western self in relation to an allegedly inferior non-Western other. Indeed, the academic study of the Orient in fact created its field of study, its object, by forcing together many varied cultures as simply 'non-Western'. Philosophically speaking, orientalism begins by assuming that there is a radical distinction between East and West, and then proceeds to treat everything as evidence to back up this assumption. New evidence can never be entirely new, because all it can possibly do is confirm the basic distinction orientalism has already created. It is, then, more revealing to see how orientalism fits together as a consistent way of thinking, than to decide if orientalism is somehow actually accurate in its descriptions of the East. Indeed, orientalism tells us less about the Orient than it does about the West. If we look at what else the West was doing at the same time as studying the Orient, we see colonial expansion and domination, and this is not mere coincidence: Said argues that orientalism created an object that could be manipulated for political and economic purposes.

Bhabha finds Said's argument very helpful, but he wants to ask certain supplementary questions about colonial power. He is interested in a psychoanalytic approach to that power, and his work suggests that colonial discourse only *seems* to be successful in its domination of the colonized. Underneath its apparent success, this discourse is secretly marked by radical anxiety about its aims, its claims, and its achievements. So, we might ask the question, 'What does colonial discourse want?' The answer seems to be, it wants only domination of the colonized. This domination depends on the assertion of difference: the colonized are inferior to the colonizers. However, colonial authority secretly – rather, *unconsciously* – knows that this supposed difference is undermined by the real sameness of the colonized population. This unconscious knowledge is disavowed: sameness is simultaneously recognized and repudiated. Importantly, the tension between the illusion of difference and the reality of sameness leads to anxiety. Indeed, for Bhabha colonial power is anxious, and never gets what it wants – a stable, final distinction between the colonizers and the colonized. This anxiety opens a gap in colonial discourse – a gap that can be exploited by the colonized, the oppressed. As I have suggested, this emphasis on agency is Bhabha's originality, as his close readings seek out moments when the colonized resisted the colonizer, despite structures of violence and domination. According to Bhabha, Said minimizes spaces of resistance by producing a picture of the West endlessly and brutally subjugating the East. We should listen to the subaltern voice – the voice of the oppressed peoples falling outside histories of colonialism.

None the less, Bhabha is following Said's thought very closely: Bhabha's post-colonial criticism merely shifts our focus, so we see both colonizer and colonized. Like Said, Bhabha suggests that traditional ways of thinking about the world have often been complicit with long-standing inequalities between nations and peoples. His work operates on the assumption that a traditional philosophical sense of the relationship between one's self and others, between subject and object, can be very damaging in its consequences – something we see too often in the encounter between different cultures. If you know only too well where your identity ends and the rest of the world begins, it can be easy to define that world as other, different, inferior, and threatening to your identity and interests. If cultures are taken to have stable, discrete identities, then the divisions between cultures can always become *antagonistic*.

SELF AND OTHER

In *The Location of Culture* (1994), a collection of his most important essays, Bhabha creates a series of concepts that work to undermine the simple polarization of the world into self and other. As the most famous example of these concepts, Bhabha's writing emphasizes the *hybridity* of cultures, which on one level simply refers to the mixedness, or even 'impurity' of cultures – so long as we don't imagine that any culture is really *pure*. This term refers to an original mixedness within every form of identity. In the case of cultural identities, hybridity refers to the fact that cultures are not discrete phenomena; instead, they are always in contact with one another, and this contact leads to cultural mixed-ness. Many literary writers have taken an interest in expressing hybrid cultural identities and using hybrid cultural forms – for example, novelist Salman Rushdie. Additionally, many non-literary writers like sociologists and anthropologists have explored this emphasis. Their writings undermine any claims to pure or authentic cultural identities or forms. But Bhabha insists less on hybridity than on *hybridization*; in other words, he insists on hybridity's ongoing process. In fact, for Bhabha there are no cultures that come together leading to hybrid forms; instead, cultures are the consequence of attempts to still the flux of cultural hybridities.

Instead of beginning with an idea of pure cultures interacting, Bhabha directs our attention to what happens on the borderlines of cultures, to see what happens in-between cultures. He thinks about this through what he calls the *liminal*, meaning that which is on the border or the threshold. The term stresses the idea that what is in-between settled cultural forms or identities – identities like self and other – is central to the creation of new cultural meaning. To give privilege to liminality is to undermine solid, authentic culture in favour of unexpected, hybrid, and fortuitous cultures. It suggests that the proper location of culture is between the overly familiar forms of official culture. Because Bhabha focuses on signification (the creation of meaning) rather than physical locations (borders between nations), his position has been dismissed as idealistic and unrealistic. However, when he refers to the location of culture, this location is not metaphorical as opposed to literal. Instead, the location is both spatial and temporal: the liminal is often found in particular (post-colonial) social spaces, but also marks the constant process of creating new identities (their open-endedness or their 'becoming'). Hybridity and liminality do not refer only to space, but also to time: one assumption that Bhabha's work undermines is the idea that people living in different spaces (for example, nations or whole continents) are living at different stages of 'progress'.

The emphasis on hybridity and the liminal is important because colonial discourses have often set up distinctions between pure cultures. Colonial power, for Bhabha, worked to divide the world into self and other, in order to justify the material inequalities central to colonial rule. When Bhabha comes to study colonial power, he argues that it is necessary to do something different. In other words, to continue thinking in terms of self and other, but simply to reverse the value of self and other so that the colonizer becomes morally inferior, is not a productive approach and in fact does not offer any real change. For example, to challenge the oppression of women by merely turning the tables and oppressing men instead is not going to offer any long-term solutions for anyone. This is just as true of the legacies of colonialism and racism. As I have suggested, Bhabha's approach highlights the ways colonialism has been much more than the simple domination of one group by another. He stresses the unexpected forms of resistance that can be found in the history of the colonized, and the equally unexpected anxieties that plagued the colonizer despite his apparent mastery. Most often, he achieves these ends simultaneously, by picking on one phenomenon in which both colonizer and colonized participated, such as the circulation of colonial stereotypes.

In offering his account of colonialism, Bhabha is transforming our sense of both the method of study and the object of study. Bhabha's project does not limit itself to the study of colonialism. In the same way as do post-structuralist thinkers, Bhabha challenges and transforms our ideas of what it means to be *modern*. Particularly in his later work, he extends his analysis to modernity in general – the ideas of scientific and material progress that mark the modern West, and are expressed in its globalized culture. In fact, it would be misleading to think of the study of colonialism as in any way narrow or of interest only to historians. Bhabha's point is that we need to look again at modernity using perspectives drawn from the experiences of colonized people – he argues that we need a post-colonial perspective on modernity, and that modernity and post-colonialism are inescapably connected. He writes:

Our major task now is to probe further the cunning of Western modernity, its historical ironies, its disjunctive temporalities, its much-vaunted crisis of representation. It is important to say that it would change the values of all critical work if the emergence of modernity were given a colonial and post-colonial genealogy. We must never forget that the establishment of colonized space profoundly informs and historically contests the emergence of those so-called post-Enlightenment values associated with the notion of modern stability. (CSP: 64)

Colonialism has been a hidden presence shaping Euro-American power and the grand narratives of modern progress. The narratives of modernity seem to be coherent and serene in their self-confidence, telling of democratic and technological progress. However, that coherence and serenity are bought at the expense of denying historical reality. Modernity has repressed its colonial origins, and, in a sense, Bhabha's project is the necessary analysis of modernity to uncover this repression. It is in fact like the psychoanalysis of modernity, an idea that will seem initially confusing, given that we usually think psychoanalysis is the analysis of individuals rather than groups, nations, etc. However, psychoanalysis is concerned with interpreting stories, and groups have their own stories, just like the stories of the analysed patient. In fact, psychoanalysis suggests all identities are incomplete, whether they are individual or collective identities. This incompleteness is not a problem to be solved, and we could never in principle have a full or complete identity. Instead, the incompleteness of identity needs to be acknowledged. So, modernity has seemed to be stable, with its own coherent narratives of progress. Instead, we should see modernity as something that needs to be hybridized: there are many ways to understand the modern world, and many contributions that have been ignored, which we now need to acknowledge and explore. Bhabha's project foregrounds modernity's complex hybridity.

THIS BOOK

The structure of this book is chronological, ending with Bhabha's more recent application of his ideas to the context of human rights issues. In each case, chapters explore ideas found in *The Location of Culture*, illustrating them with Bhabha's many varied writings on art, photography, cinema, and so on. In several chapters the ideas are applied in more detail to the reading of specific literary texts. The book works through various key terms, building a sense of Bhabha's work that begins with his essential method, and moves on to look at different applications of this method in various colonial and post-colonial contexts.

The next chapter, 'Reading', gives an outline of Bhabha's influences in the work of post-structuralist thinkers Jacques Derrida and Michel Foucault. It moves on to look at examples of Bhabha's post-structuralist reading method, his interpretations of John Stuart Mill and Frantz Fanon. Following that, the chapter on 'The Stereotype' looks at how Bhabha reinterprets the discourses of colonialism, finding an anxiety central to the discourses of the colonizer. This idea of anxiety is developed further in the next chapter, on 'Mimicry', which examines the ways that the colonized retain their power to act despite the apparent domination of the colonizer. These two chapters explain Bhabha's early work on colonialism. The chapters that follow explain the contemporary applications of his ideas. The chapter on 'The Uncanny' explains how Bhabha uses psychoanalytic categories to understand colonialism and post-colonialism: in particular, the idea of the uncanny structures both Bhabha's theory of colonial identity and his post-colonial perspective on the present. This conceptual structure is extended in Chapters 6 and 7, which follow the implications of hybridity for discourses of nationalism and cultural rights. Bhabha's work can be applied to nations and to what is beyond nations – transnationalism and globalization. These chapters together show how Bhabha's thought transforms our ideas about nations and, increasingly, transnationalism or globalization. They point to future directions in Bhabha's ideas. Finally, Chapter 8, 'After Bhabha', explains positive and negative responses to Bhabha's work, suggesting ways people have either contested or transformed Bhabha's analyses. The section on 'Further reading' gives detailed bibliographic information on Bhabha's writings, and on related texts, allowing exploration of his ideas in greater depth.

Each chapter maintains a balance between on the one hand fully contextualizing Bhabha's ideas, emphasizing the ways that we cannot simply extract his concepts and apply them elsewhere, and on the other hand cutting through that contextual information to give you a logical core and method for reading any text. It is an evident paradox of Bhabha's status that, despite his influence on so many thinkers from art history to legal studies, much of his most influential work is apparently strictly and narrowly situated within colonial literature and other forms of colonial archive. To explain how this apparent paradox comes about, I will first introduce Bhabha's reading method.

2

READING

INTRODUCTION

This chapter explains how Bhabha approaches theoretical, historical, and literary texts. It looks at his reading method, the texts he reads with this method, and our experience of reading his own texts. Bhabha's criticism is important because of his attention to anxiety and agency, but a key point is that he finds their traces through his reading methods. This chapter, and the next, are about the key influences on Bhabha and how he has used and developed them. Critically, he has developed their models of reading in directions that are initially surprising. In one interview Bhabha says: 'I am really of the school of reading as ravishment, reading as being ravished.' (ST: 373) Reading is both ravishing the text and being ravished in return. What do these two forms of ravishment mean? This chapter will answer this question by first looking at Bhabha's own prose. It then turns to look at the way this critical thinking works in relation to liberal political traditions. From here, it turns to the relation between critical thinking and Marxist traditions, and focuses on Bhabha's reading of another central influence, Frantz Fanon. Throughout I suggest that Bhabha can be read poetically.

As I will suggest, many complexities in reading Bhabha's work derive from its poetic qualities: it is unsurprising that he once aspired to be a poet. The modes of reading to which Bhabha is attracted are literary: they are literary critical, attentive to language and its ambiguities, hesitations, excesses, and silences. His readings of other writers, from many different contexts and disciplines, have this literary quality in common. This quality can cause difficulties because colonialism seems more a matter of political and legal documents than poems, plays, and novels. Bhabha seems to be making a 'category error', applying inappropriate reading techniques to the texts of colonialism. Additionally, the meanings of Bhabha's own texts can be elusive. They seem to be constantly undermining or frustrating meaning, never quite susceptible to being pinned down: just when you think you have got him fixed, the meaning seems to change. As he says himself, however, this sense of frustration involves the reader in his work: 'The reader, for me, must feel engaged at all levels of witnessing, in the very midst of unfolding of a theoretical idea. For me, writing is really a contingent and dramatic process.' (ST: 372) Bhabha does not think that his ideas, or anyone else's, will be transparently available for simple transmission to a passive readership. Bhabha's literariness in his reading and writing, and the active engagement it requires of his readers, is central to understanding his work, as this chapter will show.

READING BHABHA

As the opening chapter mentioned, this book outlines key ideas from Bhabha's work, putting them in the conceptual and historical context. This is particularly useful for Bhabha because reading him can be initially confusing. His essays are complex, fragmented mosaics of quotation, neologism, poetry, and cultural analysis. Further, they are not coherent mosaics in which all the pieces fit together harmoniously: their pieces often have jagged edges. They are mixed critical texts that use concepts or quotations in a patchwork critical form. This kind of writing requires a straightforward introduction, which this book provides; however, this does not mean that you should avoid reading Bhabha's original writing, which has its own poetic logic.

I want to foreground one particular explanation of how Bhabha writes. It comes from the work of political psychologist Ashis Nandy (1937–). He suggests that the way we write cultural criticism has its own political significance, especially when that culture is as politically charged as colonial culture. Nandy proposes that 'The first identifier of a post-colonial consciousness cannot but be an attempt to develop a language of dissent which would not make sense – and will not try to make any sense in the capitals of the global knowledge industry.' (1998: 147) Nandy's point is that Western knowledge is not necessarily a desirable end, converging as it has done with various dubious attitudes (towards the non-white, women, children, the environment, animals, and so on); accordingly, post-colonial knowledge should not aim to fit within the parameters of Western knowledge. A post-colonial form of knowledge might well seem 'non-sense', depending on where you are standing. Indeed, Bhabha's difficult style would then be a particularly suitable way to write post-colonial criticism and theory. It is helpful to keep this kind of argument in mind when you read Bhabha.

Bhabha's work does not pretend to be poetry as such, but it shows poetic qualities. It incorporates a range of styles, juxtaposing historical descriptions, psychoanalytic analogy, and literary criticism. This is not inappropriate, for philosophy, economics, history, and so on, all have long histories of writers who explore the rhetorical possibilities of the languages in which they have written. Further, poets and novelists have often done 'the reverse', incorporating elements of philosophy, economics, and history in their work. Bhabha's writing is profitably understood as working in this exploratory manner. Indeed, many of the writers by whom Bhabha is influenced also write in this way, and it is to some of these writers that I will now turn.

BHABHA READING

Among others, Bhabha has developed his ideas from the work of M. M. Bakhtin (1986), Antonio Gramsci (1971), Hannah Arendt (1951;

1958), W. E. B. Du Bois (1995), and Albert Memmi (1965; 2000). His influences are so numerous that I will focus on two of Bhabha's key influences, Jacques Derrida and Michel Foucault, and on Bhabha's development of his sense of critical thinking as a process. Looking at how Bhabha reads these two thinkers, and particularly at the model of reading drawn from their work, will usefully introduce how he reads generally.

Two terms will help get to the core of Bhabha's reading method – 'iteration' and 'the statement'. The former comes from Derrida, the latter from Foucault. Iteration refers to the necessary repeatability of any mark, idea, or statement if it is to be meaningful. A mark that could occur only once would be meaningless (for example, a squiggly line that I claimed replaced '0': unless it was repeated and accepted, it would not mean what I said). Iteration – repeatability or iterability – is one of the processes from which meaning derives. However, this repeatability is not just the simple reproduction of identical marks in other times and places. Importantly, the repetition means that those marks, the statement, must reappear in different contexts: those contexts change what the statement means. 'I love you' is one example, a cliché because of its overuse, and because it always seems unoriginal. At the same time, however, it will continue to be spoken and written

Born in Algeria, **Jacques Derrida** was a French philosopher best known for his *deconstruction* of the Western philosophical tradition. By deconstruction is meant, among other things, showing how apparently simple binary oppositions – for example presence as opposed to absence, or speech as opposed to writing – are in fact extremely complex. This aspect of Derrida's work is important to Bhabha, who finds that the oppositions of colonizer/colonized or metropolis/colony are also complicated and interwoven. Derrida's thinking is concerned with the 'absolutely other', with what is beyond thought. His *Of Grammatology* (1967) argues that the opposition between speech and writing has been central to Western thought: where speech is alive, flexible, and has the speaker present, writing is dead, concrete, only existing because the speaker cannot be everywhere to state his or her message (speakers are finite beings). This assumption goes hand in hand with a rejection of the 'other'. However, Derrida argues that 'speech' and 'writing' are, in fact, more similar

than different: essentially, he sees the traditional characteristics of writing operating in speech as well. In fact, much of Derrida's work has been concerned
with writing, and philosophies of language, yet Derrida is not a philosopher of
language, but a philosopher through language: his writings strive for literary
effects, with meaning beyond what can be formalized in a system, and in this
too his influence on Bhabha is clear. Various key terms in Bhabha can be
traced back to Derrida: iteration, writing, difference, and deferral.

Michel Foucault was a French thinker whose work focused on the history of systems of thought. His early work looked at how madness (1965), medicine (1973)
and prisons were understood (1978), and how these understandings changed
over time. For example, in the eighteenth century criminals were punished by
physical pain and torture, yet by the beginning of the nineteenth century, they
were imprisoned. For Foucault, this change suggests that how the body was
treated and what people thought was human (and 'humane') had changed radically. Foucault's later writings are an ambitious history of sexuality, tracing constructions of the self from classical antiquity to the present; these writings tend
towards intricate, highly detailed 'micrological' studies, as opposed to larger
macro-scale political or economic studies (1985; 1986). Central to all his work is
what he called 'discourse': the deeper ideas that lie behind the ideas we take for
granted, the structures that enabled any thought whatsoever (1981). In any
given moment, then, he often finds parallels between apparently different disciplines: there is more in common between biology and economics at one time,
than there is in biology over a period of time, or between two kinds of biology
either side of a radical change or 'epistemological break' (1970). Although
Foucault himself does not often discuss colonialism, his work on discourse has
been central to postcolonial theory, inspiring Edward Said's analysis of orientalism as a discourse, which I discuss further in the next chapter.

around the world for a long time to come, always meaning the same
thing but also something slightly different every single time.

Bhabha situates the Derridean idea of iteration in the context of
the 'statement'. This is a term with a specific meaning that he takes
from the work of Foucault, another great influence. Foucault
explored how disciplines, bodies of knowledge and institutions –

many of the most important of which have been colonial – developed. His work helps us analyse 'colonial statements' – statements that make up colonial discourse. We usually feel we know what a statement means, but this feeling only arises because we know the context in which it is made, how it fits in with a body of knowledge. These understandings are, however, always imperfect, as Bhabha remarks: 'any change in the statement's conditions of use and reinvestment, any alteration in its field of experience or verification, or indeed any difference in the problems to be solved, can lead to the emergence of a new statement: the difference of the same.' (LC: 22) That is, the meaning of a statement can change as its context, or the function it is intended to perform, changes. This is a difference which comes about through iteration, and it is something Bhabha finds in many colonial statements. His reading method is alive to the subtle differences in meaning that colonial authority is unable to control because of the logic of iteration.

READING CRITICAL THINKING

Following this logic of iteration, Bhabha develops a distinct idea of critical thinking. Critical positions do not, on this iterative logic, stand external to the situation under consideration: one cannot simply 'apply' a critical position to a situation like a mathematical formula. Just as in the case of a stereotype (see Chapter 3), the fact that statements only seem to have a fixed meaning, or that their stabilization is an uncertain, hesitant product of disciplinary processes, has implications for the study of statements and the discourses of which they are part.

Bhabha writes of critical thinking as a *process*, rather than the adoption of pre-arranged, pre-determined positions; he refers to 'the boundary and location of the event of theoretical critique which does not *contain* the truth'. (LC: 22) The critique he has in mind, which is always marked by being a process rather than a procedure, is just as ambivalent as the colonial discourse that is his first object of study. If we already know exactly what we think before we start reading anything, then we never quite start reading the thing itself: we merely find what we expected, and our expectations are likely to be confirmed. A reading procedure like this is just as set on stabilizing itself as colonial discourse, and is just as marked by its uncertainties. So, Bhabha writes the following:

> The 'true' is always marked and informed by the ambivalence of the process of emergence itself, the productivity of meanings that construct counter-knowledges *in media res*, in the very act of agonism [struggle], within the terms of a negotiation (rather than a negation) of oppositional and antagonistic elements. Political positions are not simply identifiable as progressive or reactionary, bourgeois or radical, prior to the act of *critique engagée*, or outside the terms and conditions of their discursive address. (LC: 22)

He is arguing that political positions are always in context, in relation to specific debates and issues, and are not, therefore, 'left' or 'right' outside specific situations. It is often said that politics is the art of the possible. Utopian political projects – Marxism, for example – are often said to fail to take account of practical political realities, with their unrealistically pure proposals coming from an imaginary external position. We are enjoined to *be realistic*, and to think about the messy practicalities of our political lives. Although this latter position is not quite Bhabha's ('be realistic' merely reverses the terms of utopian political visions and says that our present situation is as good as things will ever get), it has a similar emphasis on messiness and hybridity. Bhabha acknowledges that the middle of things is simply where we find ourselves, and no amount of elaborate thinking will ever get us out of this contingent situation, so we had better get used to working at our projects with no absolute guarantees, no final assurances, and no excessive rigidity of purpose. What we have is likely to become clear only after the fact, if at all.

That might sound as if Bhabha has no principles, but it is better to think about a lack of finality: whatever principles one has are not quite final, nor could they ever be as they are always in the middle of a particular situation. In 'The Commitment to Theory' he makes clear that the definition of principles, and political objects towards which to work or owe allegiance, is important and valid; these principles and objectives he thinks of as 'activist'. However, he also feels that there is another option, the 'theorist' option, with different 'operational qualities'. (LC: 21) This option works alongside activism. If this is a division of labour, then the theorist has the time to devote to the knotty difficulties of thought which is always on the move and self-revising. After all, the construction of political subjectivity, of any type, is from the beginning caught up in untidy and contingent process:

> 'What is to be done?' must acknowledge the force of writing, its metaphoricity and its rhetorical discourse, as a productive matrix which defines the 'social' and makes it available as an objective of and for, action. Textuality is not simply a second-order ideological expression or a verbal symptom of a pre-given political subject. (LC: 23)

That is, for Bhabha, when we come to make political decisions we are not acting on some pre-existent object called society or the social. The social is something that is constructed through forms of shaping rhetoric and discourse: he uses Derrida's term for this, 'metaphoricity', the sense that a metaphor has an ability not only to describe but also to shape or even to prescribe. For example, if we follow the metaphor 'a city is a living organism' to its logical implications, then various questions follow: are certain parts of the organism diseased, dying or dead, and what happens to the people living in those parts? In the context of the social, metaphoricity has important consequences for political thinking. For Bhabha, as for Derrida, the social is something inflected by language's slips and hesitations. Accordingly, to have a full sense of the social the theorist needs to attend to language *as* language, with all its accompanying difficulties. The theorist, for Bhabha, is very much on the side of writing.

It is also from this, in part, that Bhabha develops his sense of 'the subject'. Just as there is no pre-existent object called society, or the social, there is no simple pre-given subject. Subjects, of course, act on objects. However, what is done constructs the subject as much as the subject does it: the situation affects the subject, just as much as the subject acts upon the situation. So, in the sentence, 'the men hunt the elephant', the men could be 'the elephant-hunters', defined by their actions. Moreover, as we cannot control many of the things that happen to us, critics often refer to the subject as *constructed*. For example, we have no choice about our place of birth, and this plays a role in our 'subjectivity' or sense of identity, for example constructing us as Japanese subjects prior to our individual choices. Choices made by other people construct our identities, and our own choices in turn construct and transform our identities: our day-to-day activities continue this process of construction. If we think about this construction in terms of politics, we can say that we are simultaneously actors, making political choices, and objects, the results of those choices: as subjects we both create and are created. In this way, subjectivity is always in process, and our subjective identities never take on the fixedness and solidity of objects. Bhabha writes that 'The epistemological distance between subject and object, inside and outside, that is part of the cultural binarism that emerges from relativism, is now replaced by a social process of enunciation.' (PA: 57) Critical thinkers want to understand subjective identities, but if they could ever fix those identities, in other words make them objective, then subjects would no longer be subjects at all, and there would be no one left to want to know. To be a knower is to be in process.

So, Bhabha's understanding of the logic of iteration, and the subjectivity it implies, leads him to a specific sense of critical thought as a matter of process. Further, Bhabha's ideas about this critical thinking make him question two major traditions of political thought, liberalism and Marxism, and it is to these traditions that I now turn.

POLITICAL READING: LIBERALISM AND MILL

John Stuart Mill (1806-1873) was one of the most important British philosophers of the nineteenth century, and also an administrator in British India. His most famous works are 'On Liberty' (1859) and 'Utilitarianism' (1861). Among other topics, he is associated with political economy, utilitarian philosophy, and liberalism. Bhabha is interested in Mill's liberalism and utilitarianism in particular. For liberal philosophy, the only justification for political organizations is the serving of individual interests. This combines with utilitarianism – the principle of utility, according to which the objective happiness of the greatest number of people is central. For Mill, our rights are based on the happiness that comes from pursuing our deepest unchanging interests. So, we are free to pursue our individual interests, except when those interests interfere with the permanent interests of other individuals. For Mill, then, liberty is defined in negative terms: it means *to be left alone*. Further, this idea of liberty means that political interaction takes place between already well defined individual subjects.

In his essay 'The Commitment to Theory', Bhabha analyses a famous and influential essay, 'On Liberty' by John Stuart Mill. In Bhabha's analysis, the creation of a political subject, the subject of the political process, is 'a discursive event'. (LC: 23) Exactly what this means will show how Bhabha reads and why reading is so important in his project; it will also show Bhabha's understanding of the liberal tradition. Mill's essay is a classic statement of British liberalism, defending the right of all individuals to pursue their own aims in their own ways, so long as those ways do not impede the legitimate interests of others. Mill was not only a philosopher, but was also actively involved in the administration of the East India Company, and the connection between these two aspects of his life makes him an important figure for Bhabha's model of colonial discourse analysis. Bhabha looks specifically at the chapter 'On the Liberty of Thought and Discussion', which tries to formulate a public rhetoric adequate to fair conversational or dialogical exchange, in other words a rhetoric which would work for the necessarily ongoing day-to-day business of politics. Indeed, Bhabha argues that it is 'here [in a foundational liberal text] that the myth of the "transparency" of the human agent and the reasonableness of political action is most forcefully asserted'. (LC: 24) However, Bhabha quotes one passage from Mill in particular, and italicizes specific words:

[If] opponents of all important truths do not exist, it is indispensable to imagine them…. [He] must feel the whole force of the difficulty which the true view of the subject has to encounter and dispose of; *else he will never really possess himself of the portion of truth which meets and removes that difficulty.*… Their conclusion may be true, but it might be false for anything they know: they have never thrown themselves into the *mental position* of those who think differently from them ... and consequently they do not, in any proper sense of the word, *know the doctrine which they themselves profess.* (LC: 23)

Bhabha contends that Mill has followed the liberal road to a logical but unexpected conclusion. Liberalism imagines a subject which requires a worked-out contradiction: it is through contradiction and argument that we will test and develop our arguments and delineate our positions. We have to know what and how people who disagree with us are thinking, in order to better answer their charges and clarify our position. Mill's text, however, implies that this process is difficult to control, gradually taking over the subject which seems to be directing it. This process, as outlined above, seems to be endless: it is difficult to see how any stage of the movement could be finally judged, because there is no ultimate mental position from which to survey all that has passed. In fact, according to Bhabha, Mill has outlined 'the realization of the political idea at the ambivalent point of textual address, its emergence through a form of political projection'. (LC: 24) Such ambivalence is not accidental, but is inherent in the liberal political idea. To be genuinely public, the discourse of politics cannot maintain absolutely self-sufficient and fully representative political actors, acting without division or doubt and with complete transparency. Each actor or subject is divided, and each constructed identity is always split.

Interestingly, Bhabha's reading of Mill treats this split as if it was already there, waiting to happen, no matter what Mill may have wanted to say. This is a further distinguishing mark of Bhabha's reading method. Bhabha suggests the following: 'The textual process of political antagonism initiates a contradictory process of reading between the lines; the agent of the discourse becomes, in the same time of utterance, the inverted, projected object of the argument, turned against itself.' (LC: 24). That is, what underlies a political argument is the ability to read between the lines, to understand what the opponent is doing. Mill's argument (despite himself) about the political subject has the same structure that enables Bhabha's reading. So, Bhabha argues the following: 'Reading Mill, against the grain, suggests that politics can only become representative, a truly public discourse, through a splitting in the signification of the subject of representation; through an ambivalence at the point of the enunciation of politics.' (LC: 24) Just as reading finds instabilities, uncertainties, a shifting context, so too does politics: there are no fixed positions, and indeed (following Mill) instability and 'split enunciation' underlie the very political process of argument. The political subject has difference within itself.

For Bhabha, if – even in this classic liberal text – such a split is necessary, then there can be no essential identity to any political subject. This has a further consequence for contemporary political culture: 'Denying an essentialist logic and a mimetic referent to political representation is a strong, principled argument against political separatism of any colour, and cuts through the moralism that usually accompanies such claims.' (LC: 27) We cannot just assume that we have political identities based on consistent and original social identities: those social identities are constructed, and so accordingly are political identities. As in Mill, or Bhabha's version of Mill, this means there is no getting around the negotiation and construction of cultures and communities. The reading process is ongoing, and what this process uncovers in this particular example is the equally open production of social and political identities.

POLITICAL READING: MARXISM AND FANON

The splitting in the political subject that Bhabha finds in Mill does not just have consequences for understanding Mill's writing, or for understanding how liberalism worked within colonial discourse. It also has consequences for political reading in general, and especially Marxist reading. While Bhabha is very respectful of activist projects, some critics have misunderstood his position. Later, in 'The Commitment to Theory', he refers to an 'identikit political idealism' (LC: 25) that does not really think historically at all, but simply applies the same old solutions to very different historical contexts. This denial of specific histories coincides with a denial of the complexities of colonialism.

In contrast to this, Bhabha writes of the 'language of critique'. This language

> ... is effective not because it keeps forever separate the terms of the master and the slave, the mercantilist and the Marxist, but to the extent to which it overcomes the given grounds of opposition and opens up a space of translation: a place of hybridity, figuratively speaking, where the construction of a political object that is new, *neither the one nor the other*, properly alienates our political expectations, and changes, as it must, the very forms of our recognition of the moment of politics. (LC: 25)

Bhabha argues that critique, critical thinking, tends to dissolve certain commonplace oppositions, which in the case of colonialism are inherited from the colonial discourse under consideration. However, he emphatically does not think of this dissolution as the production of a unity, a higher term: indeed, he is writing expressly against the dialectical form of argument. (In dialectical arguments, one position, the thesis, comes up against its opposite, the antithesis, and these two are then resolved into a synthesis, a 'higher term' which becomes another thesis in turn; I will discuss this below.) We cannot assume that we already know what the political is, or what it means to think politically. A properly theoretical attitude, it would seem, balks at constructing theories, or at least theories which claim to account for everything here, there and in the future too. According to Bhabha:

> The challenge lies in conceiving of the time of political action and understanding as opening up a space that can accept and regulate the differential structure of the moment of intervention without rushing to produce a unity of the social antagonism or contradiction. This is a sign that history is *happening* – within the pages of theory, within the systems and structures we construct to figure the passage of the historical. (LC: 25)

Constructing theories often overrides the specific histories that are being discussed, so Bhabha makes it very clear: we are not to rush to produce answers or dialectical synthesis. We must not view individual examples as mere tools in the construction of our theories, which gradually draw in each text or history they encounter. The best way to understand this resistance to one model of theory – dialectics – is to follow his reading of another key influence, Frantz Fanon.

Bhabha's 'Remembering Fanon' makes the case that traditional understandings of the psychiatrist-revolutionary got him back to front. In order to make that case, Bhabha himself reads Fanon backwards, according to our usual ways of reading: he places more emphasis on this early work than on the later and more famous writings on revolutionary Algeria (see Fanon 1961; 1970; 1988). As with much of Bhabha's early work, 'Remembering Fanon' was revised as part of *The Location of Culture*, and what I will say here considers that book's 'Interrogating Identity'.

The way Bhabha reads Fanon is again literary. He pays close attention to the interplay and juxtaposition of different rhetorical forms in Fanon's text, as the following suggests: 'As Fanon's texts unfold, the scientific fact comes to be aggressed by the experience of the street; sociological observations are intercut with literary artefacts, and the

Frantz Fanon (1925-1961) was born in Martinique, then as now a French overseas territory, and he fought under de Gaulle in the Free French army in the Second World War. He was educated as a psychiatrist in France and in 1953 went to work at the Blida-Joinville Hospital in French colonial Algeria. His experiences in Algeria led him into involvement with resistance to French rule. Because of his involvement with the Algerian liberation movement, for example writing for the newspaper *El Moudjahid*, Fanon was forced to quit his hospital position, and left Algeria to live and work in Tunisia. He was made ambassador to Ghana by the Algerian Provisional Government in 1960, but died of leukaemia the next year. For a long time Fanon's most significant work was considered to be *The Wretched of the Earth* (1961), which famously argues for the necessity of violent resistance to colonialism. This book was extremely influential around the world through the 1960s and 1970s, from anti-colonial to civil rights movements in the US. However, the earlier *Black Skin, White Masks* (1952) has become equally prominent over the last fifteen years, allowing many critics to rethink Fanon's importance to contemporary issues through its emphasis on the psychological structures of race and colonialism. This change in emphasis has been controversial, with many critics arguing that it marks a neutering of Fanon's revolutionary charge. Bhabha's reading of Fanon, most notably in 'Remembering Fanon', the foreword to the reissued *Black Skin, White Masks*, is acknowledged as the exemplary text in the re-making of Fanon.

poetry of liberation is brought up against the leaden, deadening prose of the colonized world.' (LC: 41) According to Bhabha, the literary qualities of Fanon's writing have the effect of challenging the lifeless statements of colonialism: the poetic is itself a form of resistance to colonialism. Indeed, asked by its publisher to explain an obscure passage in the text, Fanon replied, 'I cannot explain this sentence. When I write things like that, I am trying to touch my reader affectively, in other words irrationally, almost sensually. For me, words have a charge. I find myself incapable of escaping the bite of a word, the vertigo of a question mark.' (Macey 2000: 159) This emphasis on the affective charge of language is clearly an influence on Bhabha's own writing.

But Bhabha takes much more from Fanon. He writes that 'Fanon is the purveyor of the transgressive and transitional truth. He may yearn for the total transformation of Man and Society, but he speaks most effectively from the uncertain interstices of historical change' (LC: 40). And in a later essay on Fanon, he writes that the

> ... manichean [i.e. with two entirely opposed sides] dialectic of colonial space and psyche that Fanon provides as the *mise-en-scène* of colonial violence and counter-violence must not be read as two separate, binary spaces. They are not to be sublated into a higher, third term (there is no universal man here!) because they must be read from the borderline that marks the passage between them. This splits the difference. (DD: 202)

'Sublated' is a technical term derived from dialectical philosophy, particularly German philosophers like G. W. F. Hegel (1770–1831): basically, it refers to the creation of synthesis, as explained earlier. As an example, if we point out cultural differences between two groups, then argue that 'there is only one race, the human race', this sublates those cultural differences into a 'higher' category. One way of thinking about this is through the example of the genre 'World Music', which brings together many very different kinds of music in an apparently higher term that transcends local cultural differences. In an article called 'World Music Does Not Exist', post-colonial critic Timothy Brennan asserts that World Music as a genre 'is real if only because it is talked about as though it were real'. (2001: 44) So, if different forms of music are sold in this way, and so incorporated into the circuits of global consumption, then the genre has a reality – but it is only the reality of consumption. Underneath this artificial corporate synthesis of music cultures, we find another reality – that much of this music has little in common, and some of it (for example, local devotional music) does not travel at all comfortably in the global marketplace. Additionally, of course, we know that World Music rarely encompasses the dominant forms of Western (US in particular) music, popular or otherwise. It might be argued that, instead of constructing such a dubious and unrealistic category, we would be better taking into account the local context and specificity of each musical form. We should defer the creation of World Music – perhaps permanently.

This deferral is central to Bhabha's understanding of dialectical thinking: for Bhabha and Fanon, deferral is particularly important in relation to the demands of dialectical Marxism. In *Black Skin, White Masks*, for example, Fanon responds to the universal demands of Marxist humanism in the following terms:

> What? I have barely opened my eyes that had been blind-folded, and some-one already wants to drown me in the universal? What about the others? Those who 'have no voice,' those who 'have no spokesman.' ... I need to lose myself in my negritude, to see the fires, the segregations, the repressions, the rapes, the discriminations, the boycotts. We need to put our fingers on every sore that mottles the black uniform. (1952: 186)

Marxist humanist narratives of resistance to colonialism turn immediately to imagine the transcendence of the language of race and the creation of solidarity. These narratives propose that there is only the 'human race', and that different forms of oppression – in colonies, of the working class, of women – are all the result of the same processes. Indeed, Marxism argues that any anti-colonial struggle should be seen as part of the more general anti-capitalist struggle, and should not limit itself by insisting on the importance of race. While this position may be a desirable end, Fanon insists that Marxism moves too quickly and is misleading in its colour-blind insistence on class struggle. As in the quotation above, Fanon stresses the particular historical moments and the specific cultural contexts. More widely, the book addresses the question of psychological recognition and colonialist resistance, suggesting that there is a clear problem: this is what he calls 'epidermalization', which is the thought that essential identity is found on the skin's surface. This in practice prevents recognition and solidarity, and disrupts the coherence of that essential identity's narrative. As Fanon suggests, Marxist humanism proclaims the transformation of the world generally, yet overlooks the persistence of asymmetrical relationships that are not based on class, but on other aspects: race and gender. If this is the case, then what is required is attention to specifically *racialized* thinking: in *Black Skin, White Masks* this attention operates through psychoanalysis. Here again, Bhabha draws from Fanon the need to look at each situation in the light of its particular specific history.

One of the most striking characteristics of *Black Skin, White Masks* is the previously mentioned refusal to remain within one discourse, and to stick to one approach to its defined problem. It switches rapidly between autobiographical reflection, psychoanalytic literary criticism, and phenomenology. In what is called the *bricoleur* manner, utilizing whatever tools are ready to hand, the book drops methods and concepts as it reaches their apparent limits, often returning to them at later moments. Unwilling to confine itself within a single mode of theorizing, the text is itself hybrid and impure. This formal mix is more than a choice of style: it also destabilizes any claims to being an authoritative narrative, or at least such claims as expressed in universalist discourses that exclude the question of race. For Fanon, as for Bhabha, although fixed identities may seem to offer stability and certainty, in fact they merely produce an idealization with which we can never be identical, and so in fact they introduce alienation into our sense of self. We need to break free from this alienation, both thematically and formally. Fanon's text enacts itself the breaking-free from such alienation, in its persistent autobiographical and stylistic invention. It is an example of subjective representation of the problem, which for Fanon is both a choice and a necessity: 'I have not wished to be objective. Besides, that would be dishonest: It is not possible for me to be objective.' (1952: 86) *Black Skin, White Masks* explicitly states its resistance to premature colourblind universalization, and also formally enacts this resistance. Indeed, this resistance to a 'universal view' may be explained in the following manner: idealization always takes the form not of a mixing but of a purging of 'blackness', meaning that blackness is seen as secondary or inessential. Realization of consciousness for the black *man* (as it explicitly always is in Fanon) therefore always takes the form of thinking *as if he was white*.

Famously, Fanon identifies the moment of non-recognition at the beginning of 'The Fact of Blackness'; it is a moment in which 'The black man has no ontological resistance in the eyes of the white man'. (1952: 110) There is nothing, in other words, to give the black male any solid identity when the white man stares at him. When this gaze is a philosophical one, the white man acts as if the blackness of the black man simply does not matter, when in fact the realities of colonialism in particular show just how much that blackness matters, as if philosophy wants politely to disclaim any knowledge of the practices of everyday life. So, the moment of philosophical universalization passes over the moment of epidermalization, in which the white gaze fixes the black, in fact:

> I move slowly in the world, accustomed now to seek no longer for upheaval. I progress by crawling. And already I am being dissected under white eyes, the only real eyes. I am *fixed*. Having adjusted their microtomes, they objectively cut away slices of my reality. I am laid bare. I feel, I see in those white faces that it is not a new man who has come in, but a new kind of man, a new genus. Why, it's a Negro! (1952: 116)

Fanon focuses on these moments, declaring that we must dwell in them, and work through their implications, before the realization of a universal humanity. This is because the idea of 'universal humanity' turns out to be a white or even a European identity. For Fanon, the humanist criticism of racist history still unconsciously implies whiteness as its 'Absolute' or privileged goal. One historical narrative (racist, colonialist) is replaced by another, ostensibly more correct (humanist), which unfortunately refuses to think about the crossover or complicity between its colour-blindness and racialized thought. Fanon implies that we should resist the urge to replace this narrative with yet another, at least for the present.

While Bhabha's various accounts of Fanon are persuasive in terms of Fanon's own writing, other readers are critical or at best ambivalent: for example, literary critic Henry Louis Gates, Jr (1991) remarks that Bhabha is inventing his own Fanon. However, Bhabha's readings do not pretend to be the final word on Fanon, or 'what he really meant'. At the beginning of 'Interrogating Identity', with its reference to Fanon as the *purveyor of an unstable truth*, Bhabha is alluding to a famous essay by Derrida on the psychoanalyst Jacques Lacan, translated into English as 'The Purveyor of Truth' (see Derrida 1987). In that essay, Derrida criticizes Lacan's tendency to place the analyst in the position of arbiter of truth, particularly in relation to literary texts. Following Derrida, Bhabha's reference emphasizes the openness not only of Fanon's text, but also of Bhabha's own text. You will remember an earlier quotation which referred to 'the boundary and location of the event of theoretical critique which does not *contain* the truth' (LC: 22). Here again there is an emphasis on process. All of the readings and reading practices that this chapter outlines presume an ongoing and radically open quality to reading. Whatever critics have argued about his reading of Fanon, for example, there is no doubt that Bhabha's reading is an event in a strong sense, entailing the reading and re-reading of Fanon's texts, but also a general and productive re-thinking of issues around colonial and post-colonial power and psyche.

POETIC READING

These different influences, and Bhabha's relation to liberal and Marxist traditions (he neither rejects them nor totally accepts them), mean that one way to read Bhabha is as a poet of post-colonialism, and to suggest that he has achieved his original vocation as a poet. In one interview he discusses the difference between the content and the figurality of concepts. He suggests that he cannot stay at the level of content, but must always move on to see how the figural or formal level transforms the content. He says that

> [When] I have grasped the figurality of a concept, which is also its fragility, then the thing catches fire. For to understand the concept as figure is to see not only its topical, spatial status in a world of concepts or in the structure of an argument; it is also to appreciate its tropic or metaphoric structure – the terms in which it may not be quite what it claims it is and why it may be something other than it knows itself to be. The figurality of an idea or concept is, to put it figuratively, the idea or concept on the move, in the process of practice or performance; opened up in this sense, one can work with it in a trans- or interdisciplinary way while respecting the specificity of any particular location of a body of thought or, for that matter, any unique representation of a body of experience. (ST: 371)

We think we know where concepts belong, but the figurative nature of any concept means that it will mean more than it seems to say, or wants to say. Concepts are like the statements that make up discourse, which are always iterable in other times and places. We can think of the process of dislocation described here in a similar way. Concepts are taken to unfamiliar places in the form of an experiment. What will happen is not guaranteed. It is not even guaranteed that anything will happen. But each time something does happen, when the concept is transformed or translated into a new context, is when Bhabha's work is at its most challenging and productive. As I suggested earlier, Bhabha's reading of Fanon is only the most obvious example of conceptual ignition, and its effects are ongoing.

SUMMARY

For Bhabha, there is more to reading – and to influence – than merely extracting useful information and discarding the leftovers of unfortunate texts. What the reader brings to the process of reading makes it live, makes it 'catch fire'. And the fact that colonial discourse continues to have readers indicates that people want it to live, people believe it has importance for our contemporary lives. Reading makes something happen, and in fact reading itself makes history. Such a reading practice looks to the colonial past as part of a process of thought, producing new answers to the problems of how we live now. The colonial is not locked in the past, but is instead located firmly in the present.

By looking at the significance of reading in Bhabha's work, this chapter has focused on both his writing and what he derives from his key influences. From Derrida and Foucault, Bhabha takes an analysis of thought's complexity, and a philosophical approach stressing difference: this extends particularly into discourses, and the ways in which different contexts change the meaning of terms and ideas. He has also developed a critical thought emphasizing process. Moreover, this thinking is specific to each situation, and cannot offer a 'global' answer to specific problems or issues without understanding specific histories. In his account of liberalism and of J. S. Mill's essay, Bhabha demonstrates this, and shows that, at the heart of this statement of liberal values lies an ambiguous split which reveals how difference lies at the core of liberal discourse. In his account of Marxism, he has suggested that – as Fanon warned – a rush to offer a final and universal answer ignores particular moments of colonial suffering that need to be understood and explored in detail. I have suggested that he is productively understood as a 'poet', hoping to set concepts alight. The next chapter turns to how the work of Edward Said and Jacques Lacan influences Bhabha, and how he extends and transforms some of their core ide

3

THE STEREOTYPE

INTRODUCTION

One aspect of colonialism that Bhabha reads with particular care is the discourse of stereotypes. Obviously colonialism has been a political and economic relationship, but it has importantly depended on cultural structures for its coherence and justification. Because it is not self-evident that colonial relationships should exist at all, something needs to supply an explanation for colonialism. One explanation has often been the supposed inferiority of the colonized people. Through racist jokes, cinematic images, and other forms of representation, the colonizer circulates stereotypes about the laziness or stupidity of the colonized population. These stereotypes seem to be a stable if false foundation upon which colonialism bases its power, and are something we should perhaps simply dismiss. However, this chapter will argue that their stability is not quite as assured as it seems, and that the strange anxieties underlying stereotypes can be productive for critics writing against colonialism. The stereotype is a form of anxious colonial knowledge, and Bhabha's writings on this anxiety revise traditional studies of colonialism. The best place to begin is the third chapter of *The Location of Culture*, which extends Edward Said's classic book *Orientalism*.

The chapter is called 'The Other Question', but its subtitle gives a much clearer sense of its content: 'Stereotype, discrimination and the discourse of colonialism'. It explores the ways stereotypes and discrimination work in terms of a theory of discourse, particularly drawing on Said's work. Although I would argue that Bhabha is not interested in constructing new totalizing theories that account for all colonial discourse or all post-colonial literature, this chapter comes close to giving programmatic definitions of his project. In this essay Bhabha works to provide what he explicitly calls 'a theory of colonial discourse' (LC: 66). This theory is based on the *ambivalence* he finds central in the colonial discourses of stereotyping.

Edward W. Said (1935-2003) Palestinian writer Edward Said was important for two principal reasons. First, he was, in the US and elsewhere, the most eloquent and visible spokesman for the Palestinian people. Second, his literary critical work has been foundational for writers, artists, even whole disciplines, over the years since the publication of *Orientalism* (1978). That book remains a striking indictment of Western racism, misrepresentation, and general ignorance towards the orient (the so-called Middle East), drawing on the work of Michel Foucault to highlight the ways in which orientalist discourse hangs together of its own accord, with little or no reference to the actually existing orient. At the same time, Said's most significant book bequeathed many difficult problems to writers following his lead, particularly around the question of representation, and what could ever be an adequate representation of another culture. Nonetheless, if seen as interventions in contemporary problems, rather than apparently detached scholarship, the theoretical problems are overridden by the effects Said's works have produced; in other words, Said's critical writings are just as much acts as his writings on the Palestinians. This emphasis on action, the performative, is one of the most important elements Bhabha draws from Said. Said's most important books of criticism, alongside *Orientalism*, are *The World, the Text, and the Critic* (1983), and *Culture and Imperialism* (1993). His writings on Arab peoples, in particular the Palestinians, include *The Question of Palestine* (1979), *Covering Islam* (1981; 1997), and *After the Last Sky* (1986). His memoir *Out of Place* was published in 1999.

Stereotypical discourse gets to the heart of colonial discursive power in general, and towards the close of the chapter he gives this summary:

> Racist stereotypical discourse, in its colonial moment, inscribes a form of governmentality that is informed by a productive splitting in its constitution of knowledge and exercise of power. Some of its practices recognize the difference of race, culture and history as elaborated by stereotypical knowledges, racial theories, administrative colonial experience, and on that basis institutionalize a range of political and cultural ideologies that are prejudicial, discriminatory, vestigial, archaic, 'mythical', and, crucially, are recognized as being so. [...] However, there coexist within the same apparatus of colonial power, modern systems and sciences of government, progressive 'Western' forms of social and economic organization which provide the manifest justification for the project of colonialism. (LC: 83)

Although he specifies the 'colonial moment' here, you will see that Bhabha does not in practice limit his sense of the stereotype in this way. He suggests that stereotypical knowledges are recognized for what they are, a means of practical control, and are also kept separate from the philosophical 'civilizing' justifications of the colonial mission; however, the point of 'The Other Question' is that the two are necessarily inseparable, with the one always undermining the other, the *phantasy* world of the stereotype always invading the colonizer's narrative. Normally the problem with a stereotype seems to be that it fixes individuals or groups in one place, denying their own sense of identity and presuming to understand them on the basis of prior knowledge, usually knowledge that is at best defective. This problem is of course present in colonial discourse. The colonial discourse wants stereotypes to be fixed, and in turn traditional analyses of colonial stereotypes assume them to be fixed. However, this fixed quality coexists with disorder, something unconsciously apparent to the apparatuses of colonial power, but not apparent to those who study colonialism until Bhabha. Analyses of colonial discourse that proceed to subject colonial stereotypes to normalizing judgements are proceeding according to the same assumptions as colonial discourse itself. In other words, these analyses assume a prior normality, albeit a positive one opposed to the normality assumed by colonial discourse. All forms of colonial identification need to be seen as 'modes of differentiation, realized as multiple, cross-cutting determinations, polymorphous and perverse, always demanding a specific calculation of their effects'. (LC: 67) According to this last formulation, every time we come across a stereotype, we need to look at it afresh, as a singular instance rather than just another example of general patterns that are so easily dismissed. Of course stereotypes are generally unde-sirable, but to make that claim is to say very little of interest. Although different stereotypes function in similar ways, it might be their differences that are most interesting, and so each time we come across a stereotype we need to calculate anew its effects, how it has been produced and what it goes on to produce in its turn. How this calculation can be accomplished by a theory is a problem that might just be a question of terminology, or might point to a larger difficulty in Bhabha's project: in this chapter Bhabha seems simultaneously to define a theory and deny that theories in general can really get at what he is discussing.

A THEORY OF COLONIAL DISCOURSE

This larger question will return, but here I will continue to explain 'The Other Question'. If this chapter is concerned with big theories, accounting for if not everything then as much as possible, it is obviously important to get the outlines of those theories right. Even when he is putting forward such theories, however, Bhabha remains cautious about just how big they might be, or how wide their application ought to become. Accordingly, Bhabha proposes a *minimal* definition of colonial discourse, which is significant enough to be quoted at length:

> It is an apparatus that turns on the recognition and disavowal of racial/cultural/historical differences. Its predominant strategic function is the creation of a space for a 'subject people' through the production of knowledges in terms of which surveillance is exercised and a complex form of pleasure/unpleasure is incited. It seeks authorization for its strategies by the

production of knowledges of colonizer and colonized which are stereotypical but antithetically evaluated. The objective of colonial discourse is to construe the colonized as a population of degenerate types on the basis of racial origin, in order to justify conquest and to establish systems of administration and instruction. (LC: 70)

Bhabha extends this definition by talking of colonial discourse in terms of *narrative*. You will see that Bhabha is generally rather hostile to realism, finding it inadequate to the analysis of colonial discourse. Realism refers, here at least, to narratives claiming to be direct forms of representation, for example in the realist novel. Here Bhabha directly connects realism and colonial discourse itself (a connection that he re-invokes in the context of the narrative strategies of the nation; in 'DissemiNation' he refers to 'the reified forms of realism and stereotype' (LC: 152)). If realism is not always colonial discourse, then colonial discourse is always a form of realism. In other words, not all realistic narratives (e.g. nineteenth-century novels) have connections with colonialism, but colonial discourse is always claiming to directly represent colonial reality: '[Colonial discourse] resembles a form of narrative whereby the productivity and circulation of subjects and signs are bound in a reformed and recognizable totality. It employs a system of representation, a regime of truth, that is structurally similar to realism'. (LC: 71) Despite slight qualifications and hesitations, here colonial discourse is clearly associated with both realism and totality, meaning explanations of reality that aim to define its entirety. As this connection implies, any further analysis of colonial discourse that operates in terms of unqualified realism or totality is to that extent far too similar to its object: when we analyse colonial discourse, we need narrative strategies that can capture its bizarre or unrealistic qualities.

INSTRUMENTALITY AND PHANTASY

Despite qualifying the connection of realism and colonial discourse in terms of *resemblance* and *similarity*, Bhabha immediately moves on to discussion of Edward Said, and so the implication of the novel is apparently clear, because Said himself makes some striking connections between imperialism and the novel form in his later book *Culture and Imperialism* (1993). In the passages Bhabha considers from *Orientalism*, Said conceptualizes orientalism as consisting of *latent* and *manifest* forms. These terms are derived from psychoanalytic language, although Said does not really expand on his reference. Bhabha suggests that it is this underdeveloped allusion to Freudian terms that enables his own definition of colonial discourse. Although this might seem a marginal point, Bhabha's comments about Said's view of discourse are absolutely central to his work, and explain the original contribution it makes to contemporary cultural analysis. In an earlier version of this essay, Bhabha simply states that 'There is always, in Said, the suggestion that colonial power and discourse is possessed entirely by the coloniser, which is a historical and theoretical simplification.' (OQ: 23) In general terms, Bhabha's work everywhere contests this simplification. In this particular context, thinking in terms derived from Freud allows Bhabha to test the *productivity* of colonial discourse – the ways in which stereotypes are solutions to problems, as it were. Such an emphasis sits well with Bhabha's invocation of Foucault, the complexity of whose notion of discourse Bhabha believes (and he is not alone) is insufficiently taken on board by Said.

Bhabha develops a passage from *Orientalism* that alludes to a 'theory of encapsulation or fixation which moves between the recognition of cultural and racial difference and its disavowal, by affixing the unfamiliar to something established, in a form that is repetitious and vacillates between delight and fear'. (LC: 73) This, Bhabha insists, connects the theory of the stereotype to Freudian notions of fetishism, and the connections are both structural and functional. The following discursive elaboration of fetish is given, Bhabha bringing psychoanalysis and linguistics together:

> Within discourse, the fetish represents the simultaneous play between metaphor as substitution (masking absence and difference) and metonymy (which contiguously registers the perceived lack). The fetish or stereotype gives access to an 'identity' which is predicated as much on mastery and

Metaphor and Metonymy are the two poles of any system of signs, the first referring to the process of selection, and the second to the process of combination. In making a sentence in any language, you select words from that language's paradigms, and combine them according to the language's rules. Metaphor is based on similarity ('He has a steely gaze'), whilst metonymy is derived from spatial or temporal contiguity ('William is heir to the throne'). Metaphor involves a process of selection, and metonymy a process of combination. A further important term is synecdoche, which is a subset of metonymy, and refers to part/whole reversals. Perhaps the most influential discussion of metaphor and metonymy is found in the work of Roman Jakobson (1896-1982), particularly his essay 'Two Types of Language and Two Types of Aphasic Disturbances' (1987). Aphasics (people with language disorders) tend to have problems in one of the two operations: they either have 'selection deficiency' or 'contexture deficiency'. Many critics have found these two poles very productive when thinking about wider phenomena; Jakobson himself famously associated metonymy with the novel, an association developed and challenged by many critics.

pleasure as it is on anxiety and defence, for it is a form of multiple and contradictory belief in its recognition of difference and disavowal of it. (LC: 74–5)

Bhabha elaborates exactly how his notion of colonial discourse's ambivalence transforms the problem of the stereotype: 'The stereotype is not a simplification because it is a false representation of a given reality. It is a simplification because it is an arrested, fixated form of representation that, in denying the play of difference (which the negation through the Other permits), constitutes a problem for the *representation* of the subject in significations of psychic and social relations.' (LC: 75) Through reference to Fanon, who becomes a more significant presence towards the essay's end, Bhabha suggests that 'the stereotype impedes the circulation and articulation of the signifier of "race" as anything other than its *fixity* as racism'. (LC: 75) Returning to the previous chapter, we can see that the stereotype is like a cliche, such as 'I love you', but it is a cliche that is robbed of its power to be newly meaningful – colonial discourse fixes identity, and denies it any chance of change. In his understanding of stereotypes, Bhabha is following Fanon's understanding of the fluidity of 'blackness'. One chapter of *Black Skin, White Masks* is called (in French) 'The Lived Experience of the Black Man'; its misleading English translation is 'The Fact of Blackness'. The meaning of race is not one meaning, nor multiple meanings present simultaneously, but a constant and unending production of contested and contradictory meanings. Bhabha thinks through this production of meanings using the work of Lacan, to which I will now turn.

PSYCHOANALYTIC REPRESENTATIONS

In fact, the theory of the stereotype must be rerouted via Fanon, who writes in terms of the *scopic drive* ('the drive that represents the pleasure in 'seeing" (LC: 76)).

Jacques Lacan (1901-1981) was a French psychoanalyst, famed for his 'return to Freud', which entailed a close textual, even literary, reading of Freud's writings. Lacan's readings of Freud transform psychoanalysis into a post-structuralist discourse, emphasizing the effects of language on the self. If Freudian psychoanalysis seeks to make whole the self divided between ego and id, Lacanian psychoanalysis suggests that such a goal is impossible. The unconscious, structured like a language, is the basis of our being, and the self (the ego) is an effect of the unconscious. When Lacan refers to the unconscious being structured like a language, many take him to be thinking of a chain of signifiers free of their signified objects, with no end in sight or centre to control them. In this, Lacan is taken to be applying the thought of Ferdinand de Saussure (1857-1913), who placed emphasis on studying language as a system at one time, rather than over a period of time. One of the most famous of Lacan's theories concerns the process by which the infant produces the illusion of its ego, what he calls 'the mirror stage': in the mirror stage, the infant creates an illusion of selfhood by identification with its own image in the mirror. The entire process of becoming an adult is an attempt to stop the circulation of signifieds, to give stability to the ego; to be involved in this process of stabilization is to wish return to an original unity (most particularly, with the mother), but in any case the stabilization always fails, the ego is always an illusion, and that original unity is inaccessible. Lacan thinks in terms

Bhabha may be exaggerating in implying that Fanon is a Lacanian in any real sense. However, his reading helps us understand Fanon's various analyses of the centrally epidermal nature of the colonial stereotype, i.e. its focus on skin. Aside from its explanatory power, Bhabha's reading of Lacan accords well with the ambivalence he traces throughout the various writers in this essay. It is what Lacan calls the *mirror stage* that is central to Bhabha's readings. Bhabha believes that the mirror stage encapsulates what happens in colonial discourse's stereotyping productions: the mirror stage is at least a good model for the colonial situation. Bhabha suggests that 'Like the mirror phase "the fullness" of the stereotype – its image *as* identity – is always threatened by lack.' (LC: 77) In the mirror stage, narcissism and aggressivity are entwined, and for Bhabha this entwinement also characterizes the colonial scene, the narcissistic identified with the metaphoric, the aggressive with the metonymic. This doubling is a different way of imagining colonial knowledge's ambivalence, always *both* an aggressive expression of domination over the other *and* evidence of narcissistic anxiety about the self. The colonizer aggressively states his superiority to the colonized, but is always anxiously contemplating his own identity, which is never quite as stable as his aggression implies.

Another way of phrasing Bhabha's argument is to say that visibility simultaneously enables and undermines the closure sought by colonial discourse. The strictly *visible* aspect of racialized colonial discourse of the stereotype makes this discourse a central example of the structures being described, which Bhabha acknowledges have more widespread applications. This exemplarity of visualized stereotyping explains Bhabha's discussion of famous passages from Fanon's *Black Skin, White Masks*, which in various ways stage Fanon being captured by the gaze of the white French. Bhabha summarizes his understanding in the

following way: 'In the objectification of the scopic drive there is always
the threatened return of the look; in the identification of the Imaginary
relation there is always the alienating other (or mirror) which crucially
returns its image to the subject; and in that form of substitution and
fixation that is fetishism there is always the trace of loss, absence.' (LC:
81) In other words, visual identification might always hold out the fantasy of full and stable identity, but that identity is immediately threatened by loss because visual identification is part of a circulation of
relations rather than a one-way fixed relation. If you stare at people it
might seem that you have fixed them in place, but of course they will
always look back and threaten your sense of self: in other words, self
and other are locked together. For Bhabha as for Fanon, there is no fact
of blackness, and there is no 'fact' of whiteness, not if those facts or
identities are imagined as permanent. At the moment you hope to have
fixed yourself, you find yourself slipping away yet again.

Many have wondered about how this structure translates into what
actually happens in colonial society. All the psychoanalytic language
tends to focus emphasis on the colonizer, and to suggest that the colonial discourse, imagined in terms of an ego, is split at its origin, compromised in one sense but also necessarily so: this apparent
compromise is what allows the whole business of colonial rule to proceed despite the disjunction between its lofty ideals and brutal realities.
And if that is the case, then critics are entitled to wonder exactly what
is so good about recognizing this split enunciation, because the colonized, the resisters, get so little out of this transformation. So, Bhabha
states that, 'By acceding to the wildest fantasies (in the popular sense)
of the colonizer, the stereotyped Other reveals something of the "fantasy" (as desire, defence) of that position of mastery.' (LC: 82) Readers
may wish to ask what the consequences of this revelation were.
Colonial life went on as normal, it might be countered: colonial brutal-
ity and exploitation did not cease just because of a split in colonial
knowledge's origin. I suggested that the psychoanalytic language places
all emphasis on the colonizer, but in one sense this seems like a strange
suggestion: Bhabha is quoting Fanon, after all, and Fanon's language and
concepts are at least partly psychoanalytic. However, as has been suggested on many occasions, psychoanalysis is a specific practice: some

extreme critics would say its relevance extends to Freud's early twenti-eth-century bourgeois milieu, i.e. not very far. It seems difficult to jus-tify applying this psychoanalytical conceptual scheme to disparate colonized contexts without simplifying those contexts or, indeed, pro-ducing a further form of colonial discursive rule.

CHANGING THE OBJECT(IVE)

The question of psychoanalysis is extremely problematic, and one not easily resolved. Fanon himself was hesitant in his clinical use of psy-choanalysis, and even *Black Skin, White Masks* is critical in its references (Macey 2000: 187). This difficult question can be made easier by trans-forming our view of psychoanalysis. As a hard science, or a clinical cure, it might have limited applicability, but Freud's writing in particu-lar has been extremely influential in more speculative thought. The place of psychoanalysis in Bhabha can be more easily understood by thinking about the general nature of his writing. We can understand it by considering his insistence, in 'The Other Question', on changing the object of analysis. Indeed, the title of the essay has two meanings: on the one hand it refers to the question of Otherness, but on the other hand it implies asking different questions about colonialism. This change clearly does not refer to a shift away from colonialism and its culture, but instead to a change in the way critics themselves represent colonialism. The shift in emphasis is connected to Bhabha's distrust of what he thinks are traditional 'leftist' modes of critical thinking, which he thinks use the same modes of representation as colonial discourse itself. Indeed, Bhabha's writing is itself an attempt to represent differ-ently.

To explain how and why Bhabha's writing changes the object, I want to discuss two forms of representation, the gallery and the museum. First you might think about a 'failed' attempt to change the mode of representation, the exhibition 'Circa 1492: Art in the Age of Exploration', held at the National Gallery of Washington to mark the elapse of five hundred years since the voyage of Columbus. Writing in *Artforum*, Bhabha considers the exhibition's attempt to make a straight-forward, all-encompassing narrative of progress by means of a *parallel perspective*. On the one hand, the show produces a world-wide vision, a horizontal, two-dimensional representation or map of the globe; on the other, it inserts a complicating third dimension by trying to represent each civilization on its own terms rather than from what we might call the 'Columbus perspective'. Still, we might think, it must be difficult to hold both of these objectives together, and the exhibition appears to suggest two troubling positions: first, that there might be a view from 'nowhere' that can encompass the entire globe; and second, that there are also pure perspectives that characterize each 'civilization', which might be re-activated to allow genuine self-representation. Taking only the first position, it is hardly coincidental that this exhibition was held at the National Gallery of Washington, suggesting as it does that the view from nowhere is really from somewhere quite specific. Bhabha suggests that

> What was once exotic or archaic, tribal or folkloristic, inspired by strange gods, is now given a secular national present, and an international future. Sites of cultural difference too easily become part of the post-Modern West's thirst for its own ethnicity; for citation and simulacral echoes from Elsewhere. (DV: 88)

The exhibition is not alone in its voracious incorporation of 'otherness'. Bhabha clearly sees this as a more general problem of postmodern culture, which consumes other cultures in celebration of its own multiculturalism without ever fully acknowledging the histories that have enabled that culture's present wealth. Quite simply, this exhibition is a suppression of history, not merely in the sense that it decorously passes over the exploitation that accompanied or drove European exploration, but also in its mastery of many different spaces in one. You will see this issue of the suppression of the diachronic again in Bhabha's work on the nation, which he conceives as a narrative strategy that presents itself as final, coherent, and static in its presentation of 'the people'. 'Circa 1492' operates in much the same fashion, substituting 'the globe' for 'the people', suggesting that 'we' really have reached the end of history, from which that self-same 'we' can survey the parallel historical movements of the last five hundred years as self-sufficient and complete. Really, however, this exhibition betrays a certain anxiety about the apparently inclusive perspective that can allow for each civilization's difference. Bhabha implicitly connects this anxiety with the exhibition's mode of presentation, its marvellous parallelism. He reminds us that

> There is no simple parallelism or equidistance between different historical pasts. A distinction must be maintained – in the very conventions of presentation – between works of art whose pasts have known the colonial violence of destruction and domination, and works that have evolved into an antiquity of a more continuous kind, moving from courts to collectors, from mansions to museums. Without making such a distinction we can only be connoisseurs of the survival of Art, at the cost of becoming conspirators in the death of History. (DV: 89)

Whilst a certain kind of 'continuist' narrative might well be appropriate for a restricted object like (still to speak too generally) European art, it is inappropriate for the fate of art objects transported around the world, often to the metropolis, as a consequence of European exploration and colonialism. There is no straightforward serene narrative that can encompass the tangled and violent histories of art under colonialism. It is, then, most disingenuous to imply through any form of parallelism that we can view the multiplicity of post-colonial cultural traditions in similar ways, which is what is implied by 'Circa 1492'. The exhibition therefore fails to challenge stereotypical discourses of art history, despite its best efforts.

Another example of failure, albeit honourable, is explored by Bhabha in 'Black Male', again written for *Artforum*. This example returns us to the central topic of this chapter, the stereotype, although in a different context. Here he considers a show of the same name at the Whitney Museum in New York, which through various media challenges stereotypical images of black males. At one point Bhabha talks to a black male Whitney attendant, and asks him what he thinks of the show. The attendant replies that the show omits too much, not taking into account all the different ways in which his own life both eludes stereotyping and, more importantly, eludes the *effects* of stereotyping.

Bhabha writes: 'As the Whitney attendant's remark suggests, there is life outside and beyond the stereotype, even for its victims.' (BM: 110) There is, Bhabha argues, something about the very form of the exhibition that fails to challenge the discourse of the stereotype, by granting far too much power to the stereotyping apparatus. In a passage reminiscent of 'The Other Question', he expands this thought:

> The strategy of the stereotype, as a form of (mis)recognition, depends on staging the encounter with 'otherness' in an airless space of fixed coordinates. No mutual movement is possible in that space, because relationships there are largely predictable or reactive: the discriminated subject is reduced to a projection, an overdetermined instance, while the perpetrator of the stereotype acts out only narcissistic anxiety and political paranoia. As I walked around 'Black Male,' seeing so many images of isolated black men staring fixedly at me, I felt that despite the irony and the inversions, something of the rigor mortis of the stereotype had seeped into the show itself. Without quite knowing it, I too had been participating in the stereotype's *danse macabre*. (BM: 110)

Even while the content of 'Black Male' (its ironies and inversions) seeks to challenge discourses that stereotype black males, its form (fixed photos of isolated individuals) colludes with those discourses. It is not only the stereotyping discourse that is fixed, but also the stereotyped object, whose processual, performative dimension is captured or frozen by the exhibition's mode of representation. Bhabha includes himself in the diagnosis of this collusion: the gaze of the viewer, whatever he or she might intend, also captures that temporal, performative element of the stereotyped black male. At this point it is as well to point ahead to the significance of 'isolation' here, because what Bhabha proposes about stereotyping discourses applies to all aspects of his work. There is an element of intersubjectivity that, however minimally, keeps matters open and denies the best attempts of the stereotyping discourse to stabilize its operations. It is that element of intersubjectivity that somehow needs to be incorporated into 'Black Male', although Bhabha does not specify exactly how this incorporation should be achieved.

WHITENESS IN HISTORY

As a final example, which this time begins to explain what should be done to reintroduce temporality and intersubjectivity, there is a further article from *Artforum* in which Bhabha considers the phenomenon of 'whiteness studies', meaning cultural histories, ethnographies, and sociologies of white ethnicity. If the colonial racist stereotype is a matter of visibility, for a long time the visibility of white skin seemed to be forgotten, or at least was never up for debate. Whiteness was transparent, and was not an issue for discussion. Whiteness studies place this issue on the agenda. As Bhabha observes, instead of the unspoken assumption of stereotypical racist discourse, that whiteness is transparent, whiteness studies make whiteness opaque. Whiteness is made visible for what it has been and continues to be, a strategy of authority. Whiteness seems to have a coherence, stability, and finality that justify its authority, in contrast to the incoherence and instability that explain why non-whiteness will always be inferior. Whiteness studies investigate all the ways in which whiteness was constructed, as a process, and the ways in which it continues to be constructed, negotiated, and subtly altered. In other words, whiteness is *agonistic*, which means it is contestatory and contested.

> The subversive move is to reveal *within* the very integuments of 'whiteness' the agonistic elements that make it the unsettled, disturbed form of authority that it is – the incommensurable 'differences' that it must surmount; the histories of trauma and terror that it must perpetuate and from which it must protect itself; the amnesia it imposes on itself; the violence it inflicts in the process of becoming a transparent and transcendent force of authority. (WS: 21)

White racism is something that simply needs to be opposed, and without question this has been and continues to be a vital operation. Such operation will tend to be organized around and in the name of fixed identities and coherent communities. Alongside this operation (although admittedly Bhabha can make it look like *in the place of* this operation), it is necessary to explore the ways in which whiteness is not one thing, and never has been one thing. Its authority is split and anxious, however unified it might be in its exercise of power. In much the same way as in colonial authority, there are originary fissures in white authority that enable strategies of resistance and revision. It is the temporal dimension that is the third element breaking open fixed stereotypes and allowing us to contest and construct identities in an unending process.

> What we need is a way of looking that restores a third dimension to hard-set profiles; a way of writing that makes black and white come alive in a shared text; a way of talking, of moving back and forth along the tongue, to bring language to a space of community and conversation that is never simply white and never simply black. (WS: 24)

To make whiteness opaque is not to suddenly acknowledge a solidity and stability that it always had. The third dimension emphasizes the processes that constitute whiteness. We need to restore this element of process. The restoration of the third dimension is of course not limited to this context. According to Bhabha, and following the writings of Lacan, we need to look awry at all the objects of our thought. Additionally, we need to talk and write in styles that accentuate the open and processual nature of identities, knowledges, and representations. Bhabha is of course not the first to consider the need to contest stereotypes through different styles of writing, and it is to literary criticism that I now turn, in order to measure Bhabha's distinctive contribution.

'HEART OF DARKNESS'

Joseph Conrad's novella *Heart of Darkness*, from 1899, is a useful example of stereotypes in this context. It is a story told by Marlow, as he sits in a boat on the Thames, of a voyage up the Congo River in search of the mysterious Kurtz, whose cruelly exploitative methods in the ivory trade seem to set him apart from other Europeans. Quickly we discover that Kurtz is more likely the most representative example of European colonial barbarity, for which African people are mere resources to be used. Kurtz sees through to the reality of the colonial enterprise, and his report is as simple as it is enigmatic: he famously says, 'The horror! The horror!' The novella has accordingly been understood as a powerful attack on the ideologies of European colonialism. Over the last thirty years, however, critics have argued that Conrad's criticism of colonialism demonstrates many of the same assumptions as its target. Without doubt there are some fairly stereotypical African figures swarming the riverbanks and forming just as much of a backdrop to European anxiety and self-exploration as the African foliage. Despite its clear criticism of imperialist projects, the novella works at, as Edward Said suggests, 'restoring Africa to European hegemony by historicizing and narrating its strangeness'. (1993: 198) Discursively, that is to say, it operates in an imperialist manner, its assumptions being those of the white man finding himself, or his steadily disintegrating self, in the voyage up-river. At one point in his narrative Marlow observes of a chain-gang that 'They were not enemies, they were not criminals, they were nothing earthly now – nothing but black shadows of disease and starvation, lying confusedly in the greenish gloom.' (Conrad 1973: 44) At best, the novella's stereotypes almost remove all content from Africans, denying them humanity. Elsewhere, there are much more brutal stereotypical descriptions. The question that Bhabha's work raises for us concerns the best way to respond to the stereotypes.

Novelist Chinua Achebe wrote a famous post-colonial critical work on *Heart of Darkness*, 'An Image of Africa', which was originally published in 1977. The essay excoriates Conrad for his racism and the racism pervading the novel. Achebe's essay makes two central points. First, he argues that 'Joseph Conrad was a thoroughgoing racist' (1997: 119); second, Achebe insists that the novella, as part of the literary canon, has contributed to the general repetition of such racism, referring to 'the dehumanization of Africa and Africans which this age-long attitude has fostered and continues to foster'. (1997: 120) Perhaps he does not fully justify either point, although he is persuasive about Conrad as an individual. However, the essay remains an important counter-attack on a particularly virulent stereotype, and so helps elaborate Bhabha's thinking on this question. It is not coincidental that

Achebe writes of the stereotype in terms of more general Western anxiety:

> Conrad did not originate the image of Africa which we find in this book. It was and is the dominant image of Africa in the Western imagination and Conrad merely brought the peculiar gifts of his own mind to bear on it. For reasons which can certainly use close psychological inquiry the West seems to suffer deep anxieties about the precariousness of its civilization and to have need for constant reassurance by comparison with Africa. (1997: 123)

Achebe's introduction of anxiety here pre-figures the structures of the stereotype as Bhabha elaborates them. The problem with Achebe's reading, and its apparent demand that Conrad be ejected from the taught canon, is that it seems to obscure the problem of time, which is also a question of colonial space. The main problem is that Achebe implicitly works in the same timeless terms as the novella itself. On a basic level, the question of applying Achebe's own values, to which many will subscribe, is open to question. Even if all he says was true in the 1970s, literary texts are open to use, mis-use, citation, translation, and transformation. If Conrad was racist, that does not necessarily make any book he wrote racist. Nor is *Heart of Darkness* necessarily racist because racist attitudes are voiced in its pages. Further, it is not clear that in its ongoing reception readers accept uncritically, or even blithely put to one side, the kinds of attitudes that the book contains. The spaces of interrogation are no longer, if they ever were, polarized into European and African, White and Black.

Also, recall that Achebe questions the wisdom of retaining Conrad's novel as part of the canon of great literature. However complex a notion of the canon you have, the canon tends towards a sense of the static. Canons of literature encompass the best that has been written, and that critical judgement is apparently immune to changing fashions. Rather than question the idea of the canon, Achebe merely questions Conrad's privileged canonical position on the basis that the best that has been written should not include simple-minded racism. You can think about this in terms of realist narratives, which were discussed briefly earlier in this chapter. The canon is itself a kind of narrative relating the best that has been thought and written, and also the development of that thought. If we want to challenge the attitudes that rightly disgust Achebe, we cannot focus only on the content of the canon (the stories that great novels contain, or the attitudes they express); we need also to challenge the very form of a fixed corpus of great works, which implies that culture can come to a halt.

Achebe focuses on the issue of content, particularly racist attitudes. Towards the close of the article Achebe worries that the attitudes he is attacking have even undermined words, his means of redress. He concludes by saying it is not a moment too soon to work at redressing the balance. What kind of counter-stereotypical strategy might be envisaged? Achebe's own novels, perhaps most famously *Things Fall Apart* (1958), are in various ways his own response. On one level they act as immensely detailed representations of people stereotyped almost out of existence by Conrad, even if it is problematic to see them as simply objective representations. By contrast, Bhabha's response is to look to those moments of fissure already present in the apparently monolithic stereotyping text. His brief reading looks to the authority of *Heart of Darkness*, which for Achebe is never in question. In Achebe's essay, it seems that the teaching of canonical literature is a question of reproducing the attitudes therein, so that the racism expressed in *Heart of Darkness* is reinforced. Bhabha's reading shifts the focus, and questions the completeness of the book's authority by looking to Marlow's desperate search for understanding and certainty that ends with his discovery of a copy of *Inquiry into some Points of Seamanship*. There is, interestingly, some uncertainty as to the name of the author – 'Tower, Towson – some such name' – and the book remains 'an extravagant mystery' (Conrad 1973: 71). According to Bhabha, far from being a simple mark of authority, or providing the solace Marlow seeks, his discovered book is doubled:

> The discovery of the book installs the sign of appropriate representation: the word of God, truth, art creates the conditions for a beginning, a practice of history and narrative. But the institution of the Word in the wilds is also an *Entstellung*, a process of displacement, distortion, dislocation, repetition. (LC: 105)

As with all the structures that Bhabha explores, there is something in the necessary repeatability of the book (like the stereotype) that introduces a temporal, intersubjective dimension into its being. The book seems to be an object of authority, but to be meaningful its authority must remain open: anyone can read it, and so its author has no power over its reception. From the beginning, the book's being is a question rather of becoming, which is what allows it to function at all, to be read at all, and which is also what allows it to be re-iterated, revised, and utterly transformed. Stereotypes are necessarily open to subversion and transformation, and so cannot quite fulfil their apparent function.

SUMMARY

Stereotypes function to enable colonial authority (and other forms of authority), providing the justification that the colonizer rules the colonized due to innate superiority. However, and this is Bhabha's distinctive contribution to the debate, there is a simultaneous anxiety built into the operations of colonial knowledge. On the one hand, authority recognizes its basis in stereotypes, producing prejudiced and discriminatory structures of governance that work on the basis of forms of stereotyping knowledge; additionally, colonial rule is informed by supposedly civilizing ideals. On the other hand, modern forms of Western political and economic institution coexist with the ideologies of superiority. This coexistence enables the real exercise of colonial power, but at the same time that anxiety troubles the source of colonial authority. There is a split in enunciation due to the excess over knowledge necessary to ensure the ongoing production of stereotypical knowledge about the colonized. This ambivalence or anxiety is necessary for the production of new stereotypes, but is also the space for counter-knowledge and strategies of resistance and contestation.

Further, if we assume when analysing colonial discursive acts that they always achieved what they meant to achieve, that they were total in scope, then we grant too much power to the colonizer. Accordingly, new methods of analysis and modes of representation are necessary, taking into account the partial and agonistic characteristics of authority and identity. This need is taken up by Bhabha in terms of the exhibition 'Black Male', but is also relevant to the writing of analyses of colonialism. Writing seems to have an authority that happily confirms the correctness of stereotypical attitudes, and this authority is evident in the case of Conrad's *Heart of Darkness*. Authority, as in the case of the literary canon, seems to be stable and coherent, always achieving the effects it desires. However, Bhabha suggests that authority is only ever complete if we take it at its word — something that colonized peoples obviously resisted, and that the post-colonial critic must continue to resist.

4

MIMICRY

INTRODUCTION

I have explained Bhabha's analysis of the stereotype, emphasizing
the anxiety that stereotypical representations betray in the colonizer's sense of self-identity. However, for Bhabha's analysis to illu-
minate the agency of the colonized, as well as the anxiety of the
colonizer, that anxiety has to open a space for the colonized to *resist*
colonial discourse. This chapter will demonstrate how anxiety is
matched by mimicry, with the colonized adopting and adapting to
the colonizer's culture. Importantly, this mimicry is not slavish imitation, and the colonized is not being assimilated into the supposedly dominant or even superior culture. In fact, mimicry as Bhabha
understands it is an exaggerated copying of language, culture, man-
ners, and ideas. This exaggeration means that mimicry is repetition
with difference, and so it is not evidence of the colonized's servi-
tude. In fact, this mimicry is also a form of mockery, and Bhabha's
post-colonial theory is a comic approach to colonial discourse,
because it mocks and undermines the ongoing pretensions of colonialism and empire. As one example, Bhabha makes connections
between the 'comic timing' of Jews and that of Parsis, the ethnic
group to which he belongs (see JA). He suggests that both groups

repeat stereotypical jokes about themselves, but that the repetition always transforms those jokes, and kick-starts the frozen circulation of stereotypes: joking becomes a form of resistance to colonial discourse. Mimicry in general is one response to the circulation of stereotypes.

The comic quality of mimicry is important because colonial discourse is serious and solemn, with pretensions to educate and improve. Perhaps the 'export' of democracy advocated by some Western politicians reminds us of these pretensions. Despite these pretensions, colonialism's grand ambitions are consistently undermined by what Bhabha calls, in 'Of Mimicry and Man', 'the figures of farce [or] low mimetic literary effects'. (LC: 85) Why does Bhabha refer to the *literary*? An initial answer emphasizes that literariness is often associated with the non-objective, the non-serious, and the non-real. Literature is like all those other apparently dismissible phenomena like jokes and myths: we know they have effects, but we act as if they are not that important. Often, then, we disavow our knowledge of the importance of these marginal things. Bhabha brings insights from literary theory to his analysis of mimicry, and literary theory shows us that representations construct the world as well as mirroring it. So, although Bhabha refers to 'a flawed colonial mimesis' (LC: 87), the flaw in question might be structurally necessary to representations in general, even representations not specifically colonial. But the flaw in colonial mimesis is important as it allows resistance to colonialism in general, and it is to the specific forms of this mimesis that I now turn.

MIMESIS AND MIMICRY

Mimicry is one name for these low literary effects in colonial discourse; Bhabha also refers to *sly civility*. Whatever he calls these effects, they do have a clear logical structure: this section begins by explaining the structure of mimicry. Recall that Edward Said talks about the tension in colonial discourses between synchronic and diachronic visions, between the idea that things are eternally the same and that there is continual change. Bhabha says that 'mimicry represents an *ironic* compromise' (LC: 86) between these two ideas. The figure of irony does not seem to be used in a restricted way here. There are many specific rhetorical uses to which the term might be put, but given that I started by discussing a sense of humour, the more everyday uses might be equally pertinent. It is important to be clear about the use of this term. It is, after all, italicized, and so seems unlikely to operate merely as a synonym for *comic*. The *Encarta* dictionary warns us about the appropriate use of irony and related terms: 'be sure that you use them in contexts associated with stark incongruity, inconsistency, or even folly, and not in contexts associated with things merely coincidental or improbable'. This warning helps here, as it implies a real intensity to the incongruity, meaning that ultimately we might not be able to explain it away as accidental. Something might be accidentally incongruous, of course, but the intensity helps direct our attention to why Bhabha finds mimicry so central. Not coincidentally, his essay quickly moves on to a first programmatic statement and definition:

> [C]olonial mimicry is the desire for a reformed, recognizable Other, *as a subject of difference that is almost the same, but not quite.* Which is to say, that the discourse of mimicry is constructed around an *ambivalence*; in order to be effective, mimicry must continually produce its slippage, its excess, its difference. (LC: 86)

Essentially, colonial discourse wants the colonized to be extremely like the colonizer, but by no means identical. If there were an absolute equivalence between the two, then the ideologies justifying colonial rule would be unable to operate. This is because these ideologies assume that there is structural non-equivalence, a split between superior and inferior which explains why any one group of people can dominate another at all. However, having introduced this slight difference, colonial discourse is unable to control the consequences brought about by that difference – particularly the colonized's agency that is implied by the slippages of meaning.

This initial argument suggests that the subtitle of 'Of Mimicry and Man' is deliberately ambiguous. 'The ambivalence of colonial

discourse' could mean at least two things: it could mean that colonial discourse is accidentally ambivalent, or that colonial discourse
incorporates ambivalence (needs ambivalence to function at all,
perhaps). Bhabha's work suggests it is the latter. He argues that this
ambivalence, a mimicry which is never quite accurate, undermines
colonialism's grand discourses of humanism, Enlightenment, and so
on. There is an obvious disjunction between the material effects of
colonialism and its discourses of moral and intellectual superiority.
What Bhabha is emphasizing is the fact that this disjunction is built
into those discourses in the first place: 'in "normalizing" the colonial
state or subject, the dream of post-Enlightenment civility alienates
its own language of liberty and produces another knowledge of its
norms'. (LC: 86) Bhabha is explicit about this being another form
of *knowledge*, which is a suggestive emphasis. It is as if there is an
obscure recognition within colonial discourse that all is not quite
right, in much the same way as with stereotypical discourses.
However, this recognition is paradoxically unconscious, and so is
not conscious mediation on the rights and wrongs of colonial rule,
for example in metropolitan debates on empire or slavery. This
knowledge needs to be thought of in a psychoanalytic register, and
indeed Bhabha uses psychoanalytic language throughout his work.
When we read Bhabha, we need to remember this use of psychoan-
alytically inflected descriptions.

I have been summarizing what happens to colonial discourse,
specifically its authority, 'as a result of' mimicry and ambivalence.
However, it is not quite a situation of cause and effect, which is
something to which I will return when discussing agency. The question of what happens to the colonized remains unanswered. Bhabha
continues to argue that mimicry 'does not merely "rupture" the discourse, but becomes transformed into an uncertainty which fixes
the colonial subject as a "partial" presence'. (LC: 86) 'Partial'
requires clarification: Bhabha specifies 'both "incomplete" and "virtual" ' (LC: 86): this does not mean *unreal*, because virtual phenomena still have effects (*virtual reality* is still reality), but it does
emphasize that despite its reality the subject is not fixed. The play
between equivalence and excess makes the colonized both reassur-

ingly similar and also terrifying: 'mimicry is at once resemblance and menace'. (LC: 86) Yet the question of the colonized's agency or free will cannot be clearly resolved. Is the colonized choosing to be a mimic, adopting mimicry as a deliberate *strategy*? Choice does not seem to be the right word, although there is some implication that if recognized as such this mimicry could be transformed into a strategy of resistance. Instead, it is the coloniz*er* who is haunted by his discourse. His own fixing strategies require an un-fixed, monstrous supplementarity, so that he can always invent new stereotypes that yet conform to what he already knew. This means that in a way the colonizer 'spooks himself': he fantasizes endless monstrous stereotypes that can only lead to anxiety rather than the desired certainty.

At this point it is important to give more details about the context of Bhabha's theorizing. In this essay he begins with India, as he often does in *The Location of Culture*. He is focusing on Thomas Babington Macaulay's 'Minute' of 1835 on education in India. Macaulay (1800–1859) spoke in the British Parliament about the need to educate Indians, to create an in-between or go-between class of Indians to help govern the huge country. However, this class became too close to home for the colonizer, as the similarity was not comforting: the resemblance was a reminder of the shaky foundations of racial stereotypes, and therefore the unjustifiable nature of colonialism. In short, the British created a class of educated Indians, but the creation made the British themselves anxious. Bhabha also discusses a 'line of descent of the mimic man' (LC: 87) through literary writers from Rudyard Kipling to V. S. Naipaul. Yet, as many critics have pointed out, Bhabha's argument seems more general, and this generalization is a legitimate gesture. The two poles he is describing seem present in both French and British colonialism. Although the two colonial attitudes are usually taken to be rather different, the British maintaining difference, the French pursuing their civilizing mission of sameness, perhaps the two poles are only different in relative presence. The structures he is describing are more fundamental than can be explained away by superficial historical differences between different colonial attitudes.

COLONIAL TEXT

Bhabha describes this fundamental level as one of *writing*, something I have already introduced in Chapter 2: 'What emerges between mimesis and mimicry is a *writing*, a mode of representation, that marginalizes the monumentality of history, quite simply mocks its power to be a model, that power which supposedly makes it imitable.' (LC: 87–8) As has been suggested, 'writing' is an unexpected term. Is Bhabha talking about what happens in books, or suggesting that reality is discursively constructed? Such interpretations are perhaps part of the story, but are not nearly enough. He is here again operating an understanding of writing, and text, in the manner of Derrida. What people normally associate with writing is, in this understanding, generalized without limit: reality is textual to the extent that this generalized textuality effect makes all presences not quite self-present. The 'parodists of history' (LC: 88) merely foreground what is already true of the colonizer's history: it is not as self-assured, self-bounded, and integral as it would wish to be, and its anxieties are structurally necessary. The dual-poled nature of mimicry is another version of this structure, a further example – although not just another name for, or merely substitutable for, the other. If this law of non-presence or partial presence is general, what specificity does Bhabha's location of it in colonial discourse have? This is a question that is often asked and is one that gets to the centre of controversies about his work.

Such a controversy again brings up the question of psychoanalysis, because one explanation of mimicry as a strategy would suggest that it is an *unconscious* strategy. Not all forms of resistance are actively chosen or visibly oppositional: some resistance is subtle or indeed unconscious. For Bhabha, that it is resistance at all is more important than the degree to which it is an actively pursued strategy. Further, the resistance he discusses clearly has textual and historical presence, and is identifiable in a range of literary texts, for example Kipling's stories (see Moore-Gilbert 1996). Literature is not political discourse, of course, but it has political implications that derive from its subtle transformations of realist representation: these transformations are evident in many post-colonial literatures.

One example of such transformative power working through a discourse of mimicry is Peter Carey's *My Life as a Fake* (2003). This novel begins with a real-life literary hoax that took place in 1940s Adelaide. Two conservative poets, Harold Stewart and James McAuley, resolved to undermine the pretensions of modernist poetry in Australia: they invented a poet called Ern Malley and submitted poetry in his name to the avant-garde magazine *Angry Penguins*. When the hoax was exposed, the Ern Malley scandal was widely reported around the world. Indeed, the name Ern Malley became famous, and the fictional poet gained a certain reality. The fame and reality were exaggerated further when, in 1944, the magazine editor, Max Harris, defended Malley against obscenity charges in an Adelaide courtroom. The invented poet was supposed to reveal the foolishness of Australian modernist literary circles, but the quality of the poetry itself (to which Harris testified in court) instead gave life to the poet, whose 'life' and work remain topics of discussion to this day.

Carey takes the sense in which the fictional poet became real, and extends it into an exploration of the power and paradoxical originality of fakes and imitations. In the novel, a British literary editor called Sarah Wode-Douglass, travelling in Kuala Lumpur in the 1970s, meets Australian Christopher Chubb. Over time she hears the story of how Chubb perpetrated a literary hoax in the 1940s designed to highlight modernist pretensions. Chubb himself remains convinced of the justness of his aims, suggesting that Australians are still in awe of whatever fashions come from Europe. The problem is that all this copying can only lead to fakes, according to Chubb. In conversation with Sarah, he expands on this theme:

> In the nineteenth century, he continued, energetically adding sugar to his tea, the women of Sydney would go down to Circular Quay to see what the English ladies were wearing when they stepped ashore. *Wah*, look at that. Must have one now. Whatever they saw there would be copied in one week. It will still be the same, take my word. Must have whatever fashion comes down the gangway. (2003: 30)

However, the novel constantly undermines Chubb's faith in authenticity. Even his own speech undermines this faith, as his English is marked by years of living in Kuala Lumpur. At one point, Chubb says '*Samah-samah*, all the same – fake is fake no matter where you find it.' (2003: 32) Malaysian English might seem another kind of fake: this is certainly the reaction of the aristocratic literary editor when she first meets Chubb and hears him use the phrase 'can or cannot'. However, she realizes that her first impression was wrong, as she discovers that the phrase is proper Malaysian English. (2003: 23) There is nothing definitively proper about British English: English is in fact not owned by anyone, and so its transformations in other places create their own versions of propriety. Sarah has a comparable reaction to the poetry she hears during her stay – and, as a desperate literary editor, she most of all desires a dramatic literary story to save her endangered journal *The Modern Review*. She decides that Chubb's hoax poetry is better than his authentic poetry: 'If this was his "real" poetry, then I preferred the fake.' (2003: 88) Instead of being secondary, the hoax imitations are actually superior to the original and authentic. In other words, supposedly fake or imitative language has its own life and power.

The novel extends this insight still further by giving a real life to the figure of the fictional poet, McCorkle. He literally comes to life, harassing and taunting the increasingly bewildered Chubb, even kidnapping his daughter and becoming her father in a way that Chubb's actual paternity can never undermine. Authenticity and originality do not guarantee anything, it seems. Even after McCorkle has died, and Chubb's daughter is living with Chubb in Kuala Lumpur, she defends the poet's memory and genius against the attentions of her father and Sarah. The forceful reality of the fake has overwhelmed the complacency of authenticity. Once your 'creation' is out in the world, it is available for use and mis-use: in short, it is open to mimicry and imitation.

IDENTITY AS PARTIAL PRESENCE

Bhabha's analysis of texts similar to Carey's shows how they dramatize the return of repressed aspects of colonialism. His analysis collides the official, conscious level of colonial discourse with an unofficial, unconscious, literary undercurrent. The resistance in question is therefore a *partial* presence. Bhabha suggests that the partiality of presence in colonial discourse leads to a kind of drive to become authentic: authentically British perhaps, although as might be implied this could always slide into being more British than the British. Bhabha writes that 'The desire to emerge as "authentic" through mimicry – through a process of writing and repetition – is the final irony of partial representation.' (LC: 88) This desire is not only that of the colonized but clearly also that of the colonizer – as I have already suggested, colonial discourse at once demands both similarity and difference in the figures of the colonized, but additionally colonial discourse's ambivalence has the strange effect of making the British feel not quite British, alienated from what they must believe is their true identity. So, when we think of colonial discourse we should not assume that this is simply the colonizer's discourse: colonial discourse necessarily draws the colonized into its circulations of identification and disavowal.

The most important thing to explore is the consequence of these circulations. It is not necessarily a problem for the colonizer that he does not quite feel 'himself': as one example, the phenomenon of 'going native' was recognized, feared, and anatomized from the beginning of the colonial enterprise. The serious problem for the colonizer is the sense that there is no 'himself' that he actually ever was or could ever become. Remember how the stereotype functions: it is easy to see that the stereotype glides above reality, licensing disgust, disavowal, domination, and death. But what applies to the stereotype also applies here, for both colonized and colonizer: 'Mimicry conceals no presence or identity behind its mask.' (LC: 88) Beginning with the pairing of metaphor and metonymy, Bhabha suggests that identity normally operates in terms of metaphor (or at least wants to), but that in mimicry it explicitly operates through metonymy: the substitution along a vertical axis in terms of parts for wholes, a never-ending substitution that cannot reach any point of full presence. In mimicry, identity is never identical with itself.

The objection to this emphasis on mimicry as metonymy is that, while it may be true that there is no fixedness of British-ness, the

British continue to rule as if that fixedness exists. What in principle is the case does not seem to have had much effect on the practice of colonialism: even when the British are philosophizing, they are not thinking philosophically about this question. More precisely, while it can be shown (as Bhabha does with Mill and John Locke) that foundational British texts do not quite mean what they say, or mean more than they say, this anachronistic reading practice bears little relation to the historical questions most properly (it might be argued) the concern of post-colonial studies. In short, the partiality of colonized presence seems to be something that has been *imposed*. Think, for example, of the different context of Australia: the Aboriginal uncanny experience of the land is most definitely not chosen. If mimicry really is a strategy of resistance, who is going to impose this partiality on the imposing colonizing discourse? Already I have suggested that this partiality is obscurely apparent to the colonizer, but is disavowed. However, Bhabha goes further, again raising the question of the colonized's agency. The objectified figures of the colonized are more than just objects:

> [T]hey are also [...] the figures of a doubling, the part-objects of a metonymy of colonial desire which alienates the modality and normality of those dominant discourses in which they emerge as 'inappropriate' colonial subjects. A desire that, through the repetition of *partial presence*, which is the basis of mimicry, articulates those disturbances of cultural, racial and historical difference that menace the narcissistic demand of colonial authority. It is a desire that reverses 'in part' the colonial appropriation by now producing a partial vision of the colonizer's presence. (LC: 88)

In other words, the colonized returns the colonizer's gaze. A little later in the same essay Bhabha explicitly talks in terms of the *threat* of mimicry as something *strategic*: 'Its threat [...] comes from the prodigious and strategic production of conflictual, fantastic, discriminatory "identity effects" in the play of a power that is elusive because it hides no essence, no "itself".' Later still he writes that 'the fetishized colonial culture is potentially and strategically an insurgent counter-appeal'. (LC: 90) This potential can only be potential for specific colonized subjects – actors. Is this historical description (did the colonized but know it, they could have mimicked the colonizer from the face of the earth), or does it pertain to the contemporary theorizer? This again is a question of how something is read (see Chapter 2): the texts of colonial authority remain to be read, and to the extent that they have continued relevance it will be *both* as historical evidence *and* as things that might help us learn how to live right now, this minute. This is not only a question of learning from history, although that would certainly be one traditional construal. It is also a matter of recognizing that the histories of these texts are not over and done with (which is why the prefix in *post-colonial*ism does not mean that colonialism is over), their contexts not something locatable 'back there' (or, indeed, 'over there', somewhere other than the metropolis). This structure is, again, absolutely general: it is what allows marks, texts, to be read at all. But it also seems to be something exemplified by the case of colonial discourse.

THE SCOPIC DRIVE

Returning to the gaze, that returned look of the colonized, we can see that it is what reminds the colonizer (and, for Bhabha, us also) that the colonized is a subject as well as an object. If mimicry is a strategy, it would seem that it is characteristically visual. Bhabha insists on the visual as a key element in mimicry, making the connections with the stereotype absolutely clear. The returned look is both literal and figural, and forces the colonizer's obscure intuition concerning his always-slipping identity into consideration (although this still might not be a question of being conscious, or of *intending* to do anything). The 'synchronic panoptical vision of domination' (LC: 86) operates in terms of fixed identities, yet is continually forced to acknowledge change. The look is on the side of the diachronic, that constant slipping of identity – perhaps talking of sides is to needlessly polarize the situation, for they are locked together in an economy: 'the look of surveillance returns as the displacing gaze of the disciplined, where the observer becomes the observed and "partial" representation rearticulates the whole notion of *identity* and alienates it from essence'. (LC: 89) Even when the relationship between self and other seems to be one of domination, the fact that there is a relationship at all suggests that domination is not total.

In psychoanalysis this question of the visual is discussed in terms of 'the scopic drive'. Again Bhabha is using psychoanalytic concepts – 'Of Mimicry and Man' gives centrality to one of Lacan's concepts, *camouflage*, which refers to blending in with something in the background that none the less is not entirely there itself. Bhabha makes clear that such psychoanalytic concepts describe how mimicry performs and exceeds colonial authority. Visuality demonstrates the extent to which colonial and racist discourses are inseparable, which is something marked by Bhabha's rewriting of his own formulation: 'almost the same but not quite' becoming 'almost the same but not white'. He writes that 'the visibility of mimicry is always produced at the site of interdiction'. (LC: 89) Remember what Bhabha says in relation to Fanon: he is extending Fanon's suggestions about how both the white man and the black man are necessarily in a state of incompletion, arguing that to fix one's identity in opposition to racist and colonial discourse is to play by the rules of that discourse.

This discussion is relevant to the *Négritude* movement, another important influence on post-colonial criticism. For Fanon, this movement can only be a stage on the way to a fluid sense of identity (definitely not a higher fixed form of identity). It would be well not to simplify, and *Négritude* is many things, but it is not misleading to say that in its explicit theoretical and poetic statements the movement is an intentional construction of a position (of an opposite and opposing position) in relation to colonial discourse. In its intentionality, then, it is quite different from the nebulous, non-intentional, unconscious workings of mimicry. I suggested that Bhabha does not warp Fanon's meaning beyond recognition, and Fanon himself tends to criticize desires to fix identity, but the difference between the two is that Bhabha can seem to imply that this unconscious strategy (if such a thing is possible) is the best or only possible mode of resistance to colonial discourse.

This discussion has returned us to the vexed question of just how conscious mimicry might be. If we accept that mimicry is a strategy of

Négritude refers to a twentieth-century cultural movement which elevated an essential black identity and culture as worthy of pride. Originally, the term and movement come from a Francophone context, and constituted a reaction to the specific qualities of the colonial situation. The term was first used in Aimé Césaire's poem 'Cahier d'un retour au pays natal' (Notebook of a Return to My Native Land) (1939). Much emphasis is placed on the traditions and unique cultural characteristics of Africa. These characteristics became significant in the construction of identity for colonized writers. Another important figure associated with the movement is Leopold Sedar Senghor, poet and president of Senegal during the 1960s and 1970s.

resistance, this raises the further question of just who gains what from seeing identities as productions with no reference to any original reality. Recall that for Bhabha the stereotype is productive, is in process, and needs to be analysed as such. He argues here that 'These instances of metonymy are the non-repressive productions of contradictory and multiple belief. They cross the boundaries of the culture of enunciation through a strategic confusion of the metaphoric and metonymic axes of the cultural production of meaning.' (LC: 90) Are these productions 'non-repressive', realistically? They are in principle non-repressive to the extent that cultural productions of identity external to the colonial situation operate in the same way, even if colonial discourse is a particularly intense example of this representation. However, to discuss the colonial example as Bhabha does might seem a little too close to discussing it as just one example like any other. Who benefits from mimicry? I earlier quoted Bhabha, arguing that mimicry is a matter of both resemblance and menace – to the colonizer. However, Bhabha himself makes the obvious point that 'The ambivalence of colonial authority repeatedly turns from *mimicry* – a difference that is almost nothing but not quite – to *menace* – a difference that is almost total but not quite.' (LC: 91) The same resemblance/menace is turned on the colonized: now you are like 'us', now you are so other we must enact violence upon you. That the former is structurally the case should not allow us to forget that the latter case was *historically* the case. It is when there is real ambiguity about the extent of his claims that Bhabha's work is most controversial. Stereotypes are an example of how identities are mere productions, but their damaging effects and the many powerful examples of colonized counter-discourses always remind us that identities are not 'merely' anything. Identities can be lightly borne, worn, or torn asunder, only if we have legal, material and other securities (see Chapter 7).

'IMAGINARY HOMELANDS'

We need to bear this in mind when we read Bhabha's extension of mimicry into other contexts, for example that of national identity. Mimicry suggests that our construction of identity is necessarily fluid and imaginary, and so Bhabha's analysis is open to such extension, but only with caution. For example, the phrase 'Imaginary Homelands' is the title of a Salman Rushdie essay; it also echoes historian Benedict Anderson's *Imagined Communities* (1983; revised edn 1991), an account of the emergence of the modern nation that had an important influence on Bhabha's thinking, as explained in Chapter 6. What does the phrase 'imaginary homeland' suggest? In one way, to imagine a homeland is actually to imagine something very solid that will ground and guarantee your identity. Feeling like your home is elsewhere can lead you to imagine a homeland that is a pure, untainted place to start again. For example, stuck in London but dreaming of Jamaica, Irie in Zadie Smith's *White Teeth* thinks the following:

> No fictions, no myths, no lies, no tangled webs – this is how Irie imagined her homeland. Because *homeland* is one of the magical fantasy words like *unicorn* and *soul* and *infinity* that have now passed into the language. And the particular magic of *homeland*, its particular spell over Irie, was that it sounded like a beginning. The beginningest of beginnings. Like the first morning of Eden and the day after apocalypse. A blank page. (2000: 402)

With no experience of your homeland, you are free to imagine it in almost any way you choose, and to give it a well-founded and reliable identity. But there are other ways to imagine a homeland, something Smith's novel in fact does by making all homelands feel provisional and open. A few pages later, thinking of the *accidental* quality of birth and belonging, we find that, for Irie, 'the land of accidents sounded like *paradise*.... Sounded like freedom'. (2000: 408) It is possible to convert the absence of definitive identity into a privilege, which is certainly one way to understand Bhabha's mimicry. At the same time, it is important to avoid romanticizing this lack of final grounded identity, which is experienced by different people in very different ways. Mimicry is itself a markedly ambivalent phenomenon.

For example, if we turn to Rushdie's 'Imaginary Homelands', it makes the following statement about the 'migrant condition': 'Our identity is at once plural and partial. Sometimes we feel that we straddle two cultures; at other times, that we fall between two stools, but however ambiguous and shifting the ground may be, it is not an infertile territory for a writer to occupy.' (1992: 15) Such a privilege quite often, and suddenly, reverses itself and becomes a burden. In Rushdie's essay the focus is on the imaginary homelands of the migrant, which are exemplary of everyone's imagination of home. Bhabha's idea of mimicry, you will remember, needs to be thought of as a process that mimics no fixed, final, foundational identity. The colonizer has no absolute pre-existent identity which can be mimicked, and the colonized likewise has no real identity which he or she is betraying through mimicry. The homelands we create are, for Bhabha like Rushdie and Smith, imaginary, which does not mean they are unreal. This unreality implies that we can re-imagine them, in principle endlessly, although of course practical constraints often make this re-imagination difficult to achieve. It is when mimicry becomes locked into a closed economy, through which cultural identity is fixed by the colonized, that problems arise from this process.

The example that this section will consider has already been mentioned. V. S. Naipaul's *The Mimic Men* (1967) is central in Bhabha's lineage of mimicry, and 'Of Mimicry and Man' quotes a brief passage from the novel. The novel is structured around four periods of its main character's life. There is his childhood on the fictional Caribbean island of Isabella, along with his later return as businessman and politician; additionally, we learn of his student years in London, and his later return there to live in a hotel and write his life story. The novel's contexts and themes have obvious connections with Bhabha's work.

However, readers familiar with Naipaul's work and this novel in particular might wonder about Bhabha's implication that it is connected with his own notion of mimicry. To start with, Naipaul's work is infamous for elevating Western culture at the expense of 'half-made' other cultures. Further, the mimic man himself, short-lived colonial politician Ralph R. K. Singh, is singularly unempowered by his mimicry. In his account of his time as a colonial politician, his childhood island home of Isabella gains its independence, yet the British seem peculiarly unfazed by Singh's ruses, strategies, and actions. Written after his life lived 'in parenthesis', aged forty and living in a suburban hotel in London, Singh's distanced account of his actions at times becomes almost a historical and political essay about Isabella. The novel's central theme, a longing for the wider world, is expressed in the passage Bhabha quotes:

> We, here on our island, handling books printed in this world, and using its goods, had been abandoned and forgotten. We pretended to be real, to be learning, to be preparing ourselves for life, we mimic men of the New World, one unknown corner of it, with all its reminders of the corruption that came so quickly to the new. (Naipaul 1967: 146)

It is in this wider world that much of the book takes place: the life 'in parenthesis', which actually takes in his Isabella childhood and later career as island landowner and politician, is book-ended by his intervening time at college in London and his late period of writing, again in London. It is against the reality of London that the mimicry of Isabella is placed; all the immigrant characters Naipaul introduces in his student years are flat when viewed against the depth of the city itself: 'It was always good to see them, familiar in all the unknown of the city. But this was how they always appeared: two-dimensional, offering simple versions of themselves.' (1967: 14) Notably, extremely few if any of London's characters are 'British'; Naipaul concentrates on the city's others, who appear so fake and insubstantial against its mass: 'In the great city, so three-dimensional, so rooted in its soil, drawing colour from such depths, only the city was real. Those of us who came to it lost some of our solidity; we were trapped into fixed, flat postures.' (1967: 27) Lieni helps Singh develop his character of the 'rich colonial dandy', enabling a sequence of sexual predation, usually at the expense of Scandinavians, just as later Browne and Singh feed off each other in their creation of their politicians' roles.

Mimicry in the later political career is traced back to the Isabella childhood, and through the London student years. Singh's childhood acts work, 'not to simplify but to complicate' (1967: 93–4), for example in his name change from Ranjit Kripalsingh to Ralph R. K. Singh. When he decides to 'become a sportsman', despite his own inadequacies the other students are willing to play along with the illusion, the role: 'The discovery that many were willing to take me for what I said was pure joy. It was like a revelation of wholeness.' (1967: 113) However, this *complication*, striving to mimic an allegedly more substantial culture, to produce the illusion of depth, has immense consequences in the political life. The mimicry in this section of the book is not of the colonizer, but of other anti-colonial movements. The rhetoric of Singh's movement mimics other movements; it is not quite that this is false, but that it speaks too generally: 'We spoke as honest men. But we used borrowed phrases which were part of the escape from thought, from that reality we wanted people to see but could ourselves now scarcely face. We enthroned indignity and distress. We went no further.' (1967: 198) It is the emphasis on the surface without reference to substantial thought or action that leads to the personal and political crash that follows:

> It has happened in twenty countries like ours: the sobering moment of success when playacting turns out to be serious. Our grievances were our reality, what we knew, what had permitted us to grow, what had made us. We wondered at the ease of our success; we wondered why no one had called our bluff. We felt our success to be fraudulent. But none of this would have mattered as much if we hadn't also understood that in the game we had embarked on there could be no withdrawal. And each man was now alone. (1967: 200)

Naipaul's novel implies that mimicry is itself a problem. Despite Singh's dismissal of various characters' insistence that he will return to

Isabella, that it is a paradise, and that it is the source of his true identity, various incidents suggest that this position has at least the coherence that would have saved Singh in his moment of political crisis. For
example, at one point he argues with himself about a remembered
school day on which he took an apple to his teacher, although he
knows it cannot have been an apple and must have been an orange; his
memory has been colonized, or rather his mimicry has become so
deeply ingrained that he has undergone a process of self-colonization.
Is 'the truth' the true value of Isabella? At one point we see Singh as a
young boy reading *The Aryan Peoples and Their Migrations*; although this
figure might seem detached from his own island, such books suggest
an urge to bring disorder under control working in parallel with
Singh's mimicry, and it is this emphasis on narrative, on 'the first historian's vision' (1967: 81), a bringing to order, which points to the book
'itself' (the novel, and the book Singh is writing within the novel) as
an act of seeing 'through' mimicry to establish coherence. We can
think about this through Lacan's work. Recall that for Lacan, and
through him for Bhabha, the entry into language is the production of a
secure stable ego in compensation for the necessarily lost unity with
'the mother'. However far 'back' Singh might go, lost unity is still
going to remain lost, and the writing of the narrative is itself compen-
satory. Looking back to the beginning of his narrative, Singh comments by way of conclusion:

> Fourteen months have passed since, in a room made over-dry by the elec-
> tric fire, I re-created that climb up the dark stairs to Mr Shylock's attic to look
> through a snowfall at the whitening roofs of Kensington. By this re-creation
> the event became historical and manageable; it was given its place; it will no
> longer disturb me. And this became my aim: from the central fact of this set-
> ting, my presence in this city which I have known as student, politician and
> now as refugee-immigrant, to impose order on my own history, to abolish
> that disturbance which is what a narrative in sequence might have led me
> to. (1967: 243)

The novel is not a narrative with a straightforward chronological
sequence, and so it does not have a straightforward horizontal move-

ment. It is instead a narrative of vertical movements, displacements, and disjunctive repetitions: it is a novel of doubling and duplicity, something fascinating to Bhabha for reasons I will explore further in the next chapter. It is this *formal* emphasis on doubling that makes *The Mimic Men* a novel of mimicry in Bhabha's sense, even though *thematically* it accords with much of Naipaul's work in its celebration of the metropolitan culture's authenticity and solidity. Formally, the novel undermines narratives of coherence and solidity, even if its themes incline towards idealized and solid identity.

The first passage I quoted, referring to 'the mimic men of the New World', is described by Bhabha as an *apostasy* (a renunciation of a political or religious belief), and Singh is aligned with 'the parodists of history'. (LC: 88) Particularly in his descriptions of his father's mass movement and its entry into history (Naipaul 1967: 127, 141), Singh's own drive to order comes up against and is ironized by 'mystery as mystery', and his out-of-sequence narrative is only the most obvious way in which the novel is itself a mimicking parody of history. It is Bhabha's compressed reference that I have elaborated in this section, explaining why a writer whose explicit politics are often so removed from Bhabha's is yet so important to his project. Many critics might be suspicious, however, of the ease with which Naipaul can be incorporated into Bhabha's project. Generally speaking, Bhabha's readings rarely become ritualized unmaskings of writers with whom he is politically at odds: he loves the writers he reads. Indeed, this love marks Bhabha's distance from much post-colonial criticism.

SUMMARY

As with the structure of the stereotype, Bhabha suggests that the structure of mimicry derives from a fundamental but unstable urge on the part of colonial authority. On the one hand, there must be intermediaries or collaborators with whom the colonial power can work in the exercise of its authority; on the other, these intermediaries come to seem a little too similar to the colonizer, undermining ideologies of superiority. Further than that, once drawn into this economy of resemblance and menace, the colonial subject comes to undermine his own self-identical authority; repeatable elsewhere, as the mimic man, colonial authority seems to be from the beginning divided against itself. Bhabha's interest in Naipaul demonstrates how this division can be found in superficially monolithic, coherent identities and ideologies.

A further consequence of mimicry is the undermining of the colonizer's apparently stable, original identity. The fact that anyone could be 'almost white but not quite' implies that no one could ever quite be white. There are no 'facts' of blackness or whiteness (something that Fanon also argues), and this is a more catastrophic realization for the colonizer than for the colonized. The identity of the colonizer is constantly slipping away, being undermined by effects of writing, joking, 'sly civility', and repetition. These effects are in principle present in any act of enunciation, but are particularly important in the colonial scenario, with its visual element. Finally, these effects are apparently unconscious, but at the same time might become strategies of resistance to work alongside more direct and explicit action. Mimicry implicitly offers an opening for agency, and even a model for agency.

5

THE UNCANNY

INTRODUCTION

This chapter explains why Bhabha uses the concept of 'the uncanny' to characterize the post-colonial experience. This explanation draws on his understanding of stereotypes and mimicry, outlined in the previous two chapters. Chapter 3 explained that the colonizer creates monstrous stereotypes that, far from reassuring him of his authority, actually point to anxiety at the heart of his identity. Chapter 4 then suggested that this anxiety enables the colonized population to resist colonial authority through mimicry, a strategy of doubling or repetition. With these two aspects of his work, Bhabha provides a full picture of the colonial psychic economy, in which both colonized and colonizer are involved. Drawn from psychoanalysis, the idea of the uncanny is one important way Bhabha describes this economy of monstrous doubling. As I have suggested, the use of psychoanalytic concepts is central to his work, and this is because post-colonial criticism is itself a project aiming to analyse the repressed ideas and histories that allowed the West to dominate so much of the world.

For Bhabha, post-colonial criticism conducts this analysis from the margins of modern nations: they provide a privileged perspective on the apparently stable identities of modernity in general. The margins of the modern nation, like the situations of colonized peoples, should not be romanticized; however, they do offer striking resources that transform our rigid sense of the grand narratives of modernity. In their ambivalence, these margins are an uncanny echo of histories that modernity might prefer had remained hidden. Such a desire is, according to Sigmund Freud, a central feature of the uncanny. He uses the idea to explain the feeling we get when experiences of childhood that have been repressed return to disrupt our everyday existence. For Bhabha, it is possible to compare the childhood of an individual with the beginnings of modern Western history: in both cases, something is repressed but inevitably breaks through the veneer of civilization. Again, then, Bhabha is analysing the West as a patient, in search of a cure for its malaise.

REPEATING THE PAST

The first question to address concerns the privilege given to the post-colonial perspective. In the colonial situation, the marks of anxiety and ambivalence give power to the colonized agent, but of course the colonized agent is forced to live in the colony – colonialism does not allow you to simply opt out. The migrant experience seems to be rather different, mainly because not all migrants are forced into their movements: in some cases, migrancy means being upwardly mobile. Accordingly, to talk about a generalized migrant experience is to group together many very different experiences, and this needs careful explanation. This chapter will give an explanation of why Bhabha makes such a generalization.

One reason he gives the concept such power is his own experience, something that is developed in autobiographical passages. Bhabha's journey around the world has taken him from Mumbai to Oxford, then from Brighton to Chicago, and for now to Boston. But it is not only his individual travels that are important: his experience as a Parsi is also crucial. The Parsis are an Indian minority with a world-wide population of approximately 160,000; they migrated from Persia in the eighth century to avoid Muslim persecution (see Luhrmann 1996). Importantly, when Bhabha discusses his origins he is not claiming a fixed ethnic identity. This is because the Parsis are a hybrid and transnational group: 'Of modernity, the Parsis have a largely transnational experience, at first mediated by British colonialism, and later developed through a spirit of commercial and financial enterprise. On the question of western culture, middle-class Parsis, often called the "Jews of the East", have emulated the bourgeois ethic of professionalism and philanthropy, and have sought recognition in the high cultures of the West.' (JA: xv) Parsis have always been travelling and translating, then, using the language of colonialism for trade. They therefore have a hybrid identity, something marked by an uncanny ability to be at home anywhere, an ability that always might become the burden of having no home whatsoever. The uncanny, Bhabha suggests, is also the *unhomely*. (WH: 144) It is, then, connected to cosmopolitanism – specifically what Bhabha calls *vernacular* cosmopolitanism, which opens 'ways of living at home abroad or abroad at home'. (CM: 587) But we must not forget that homelessness is real as well as metaphorical.

It is this balance that Bhabha evokes through his use of the uncanny, for example in the following passage from near the beginning of 'DissemiNation':

> I have lived that moment of the scattering of the people that in other times and other places, in the nations of others, becomes a time of gathering. Gathering of exiles and émigrés and refugees; gathering on the edge of 'foreign' cultures; gatherings at the frontiers; gatherings in the ghettos or cafés of city centres; gathering in the half-life, half-light of foreign tongues, or in the uncanny fluency of another's language; gathering the signs of approval and acceptance, degrees, discourses, disciplines; gathering the memories of underdevelopment, of other worlds lived retroactively; gathering the past in a ritual of revival; gathering the present. Also the gathering of people in the diaspora: indentured, migrant, interned; the gathering of incriminatory statistics, educational performance, legal statutes, immigration status. (LC: 139)

Bhabha evokes the uncanniness of migrant experience through a series of familiar ideas. First, this is a *half*-life, like the partial presence of colonial identity; second, it *repeats* a life lived in the country of origin, but this repetition is not identical, introducing difference and transformation; further, this difference-in-repetition is a way of *reviving* that past life, of keeping it alive in the present. These figures of doubling and halving mark the experience of the colonized, as we have seen, but also that of the migrant. This passage is autobiographical, as its first words suggest, but it is also a literary performance, because it enacts the doubling it describes. When we read of 'the uncanny fluency of another's language', what does it mean? To whom is it uncanny? It is uncanny to *both* the speaker *and* the other to whom that language was apparently proper, in the same way as colonial identity loses its moorings through mimicry. Propriety and impropriety become confused and doubled. The doublings here might be troubling, as those figures celebrated in the main section of this passage seem distant from the less privileged millions remembered, almost as an afterthought, in the final sentence, and this distance reminds us that exile comes in many forms. Exile can be made into a metaphorical ideal, suggesting a positive cosmopolitan identity, but exile is not only a metaphor, and many experience it in more negative ways.

Accordingly, we have to be careful when we think about the positive qualities of exile. The idea of the uncanny is itself ambivalent, and is used in many contexts throughout Bhabha's work. All the hesitations, uncertainties, and ambivalences with which colonial authority and its figures are imbued are characterized in terms of the uncanny. For example, in a reading of Henry James's novels, Bhabha writes that the domestic and historical spheres invade each other, and 'uncannily, the private and the public become part of each other'. (LC: 9) Or, thinking back to the reading of John Stuart Mill, there we learn that, 'In a figure of repetition, there emerges the uncanny double of democracy itself.' (LC: 96) As a final example, when discussing Foucault's notion of the statement, Bhabha suggests that 'Repeatability, in my terms, is always the repetition in the very act of enunciation, something other, a difference that is a little bit uncanny' (LC: 131). Indeed, in the second and third examples, you can see that the logical structures I outlined in Chapter 2 – the split in the political subject, and the way new contexts change the meaning of a statement – can also be described as uncanny.

Everything in Bhabha's work begins to seem a little uncanny, and this is partly because of the term's general currency in cultural theory. To explain this general currency, I will now turn to the use of the term by Sigmund Freud, and also in the work of psychoanalytic literary critic Julia Kristeva, who develops Freud's insights in political directions inspired by questions of European identity and immigration. These writers use the idea of the uncanny in ways that inspire Bhabha's sense of the hybrid, post-colonial perspective.

DEFINING THE UNCANNY

'Uncanny' has everyday uses, but is an enigmatic word. *Das Unheimliche*, the term that Freud discusses, can be translated as 'the unhomely', or the awkward but suggestive 'un-housedness'. Freud's classic essay 'Notes on "The Uncanny" ' begins with its own dictionary definitions from German. 'Uncanny' is a translation of the German term, but the translation is not straightforward in either direction. None the less, I will start with the *Shorter Oxford English Dictionary*'s definition, which suggests that it is a word of Scots and Northern dialect, from 1596:

1. Mischievous; careless; unreliable. *dial.* 2. Untrustworthy or inspiring uneasiness by reason of a supernatural element; uncomfortably strange or unfamiliar; mysteriously suggestive of evil 1773. 3. Dangerous, unsafe *dial.* 1785.

This definition omits much of what is discussed in relation to the uncanny, because it cannot explore the strange reversals of meaning contained in the German, which many writers have found fruitful. The *OED*'s definitions range the uncanny directly against what is canny, cunning, worthy of admiration, and so on. Even so, canniness does not really refer to the familiar, or the good: the canny might be clever, but it still seems slightly unfamiliar, and certainly remains worthy of suspicion. So the above definition still implies various meanings found in German, at least the meanings that Freud develops. He offers this definition: 'the uncanny is that species of the frightening that goes back to what was once well known and had long been familiar'. (2003: 124) In fact, Freud makes the 'positive' and 'negative' definitions I outlined above almost equivalent. The uncanny is something we can analyse only through self-observation and self-objectification. However, as with psychoanalysis in general, the uncanny is not something that we can control or access directly – the feeling of uncanniness is essentially an *involuntary* recurrence of the old and familiar. This involuntary quality suggests that the uncanny would better have remained hidden – what returns to haunt you is actually something that you do not want to face again. The uncanny is close to what Freud calls *repetition compulsion*, which refers to the way the mind repeats traumatic experiences in order to deal with them. The feeling of uncanniness is, therefore, the feeling you get when you have a guilt-laden past which you should really confront, even though you would prefer to avoid it.

Freud is specific about how the uncanny works. For him, any repression is necessarily incomplete, and so any past is always just about to break through into the present. For psychoanalysis, the traces of past beliefs and experiences remain present in the mind. In this essay, Freud asserts that the uncanny arises from the repression of our supposedly primitive beliefs (for example, in telepathy or ghosts). We have apparently surmounted such beliefs, but this process always remains incomplete.

> Let us first take the uncanny effects associated with the omnipotence of thoughts, instantaneous wish-fulfilment, secret harmful forces and the return of the dead. There is no mistaking the conditions under which the sense of the uncanny arises here. We – or our primitive forebears – once regarded such things as real possibilities; we were convinced that they really happened. Today we no longer believe in them, having *surmounted* such modes of thought. Yet we do not feel entirely secure in these new convictions; the old ones live on in us, on the look-out for confirmation. Now, as soon as something *happens* in our lives that seems to confirm these old, discarded beliefs, we experience a sense of the uncanny. (2003: 154)

Any present identity seems to be self-sufficient, having expelled unnecessary elements like childish beliefs or attachments: as adults, we have arrived at our proper sense of self. However, for Freud this self never gets rid of these 'inappropriate' characteristics, particularly those of childhood. In fact, the uncanny or improper is built into the foundations of psychical experience, and remains a partial presence in what is apparently most proper. In this essay Freud excludes real uncanny experiences, focusing on literary examples. However, the structure of the uncanny is so similar to that of general psychoanalytic structures that the idea can be used to explain real events, individuals, and institutions. So, Bhabha, like Kristeva, is not making a category error when he uses the uncanny more widely, because Freud's own text is open to political and ethical generalization.

In summary, for Freud the uncanny contains its apparent opposite: if the canny is the homely, what is close to home, it none the less has a tendency to morph into the profoundly unfamiliar, the unhomely, which alienates or estranges us from what we thought was most properly our own. Alienation would usually be thought of as a problem, but if it is something that is part of all experience, and is even something that might inspire us to re-evaluate our identities, then we can understand it as an opportunity. The uncanny, in other words, opens a space for us to reconsider how we have come to be who we are. It is this sense of the uncanny that Bhabha develops in many essays, for example 'Articulating the Archaic', which discusses the uncanniness of *culture*:

> Culture is *heimlich*, with its disciplinary generalizations, its mimetic narratives, its homologous empty time, its seriality, its progress, its customs and coherence. But cultural authority is also un*heimlich*, for to be distinctive, significatory, influential and identifiable, it has to be translated, disseminated, differentiated, interdisciplinary, intertextual, international, inter-racial. (LC: 136–7)

Culture has a dual identity, rather like colonial discourse. On the one hand, it is homely or realist, asserting its coherence and stability: it is made meaningful by those to whom it belongs. On the other hand, it is unhomely because it is always changing: it is always being made meaningful by others, those to whom it apparently does not belong. Because culture has this dual identity, it is never quite coherent and self-sufficient. Its narratives seem stable and confident, but they always get drawn into strange displaced relationships – with other cultures, or texts, or disciplines. French culture, for example, has its own narratives that seem coherent, but depends in various ways on its others, whether they be American or German cultures, or minority cultures within French culture. This passage introduces the perspective animating Bhabha's position on nations and cultural rights, discussed in the following chapters. We can also see how migrants can exemplify this dual nature of culture, always situated in relation to both an *original* culture and a *new* location; it is to the metaphor and reality of migrant experience that I now turn.

THE MIGRANT EXPERIENCE

Today there are vast numbers of migrants who, increasingly, and increasingly speedily, circumnavigate the globe, or merely walk one hundred metres, in pursuit of income, however problematically organized and reimbursed. In addition there are those millions whose migrancy is enforced in very different ways, as they flee persecution in one form or another. According to statistics from the Office of the United Nations High Commissioner for Refugees (UNHCR), at the beginning of 2003 over 20 million people fell under its remit. The facts and experiences of migration are central global phenomena. Further, much of this migration has some connection to our long histories of travel, trade, and colonialism. Accordingly, any theory of colonialism that extends itself into the present must come to terms with migration.

For Bhabha, we can see the experience of migration as supplanting old ideas of belonging and identity, particularly nationalist ideas. He writes in 'Anxious Nations, Nervous States' that 'Nationalist aspirations turn the values of civility into forms of ethnic separatism; a sense of community is replaced by the crisis of communalism; citizenship is less the habitus of the homeland, and more frequently an experience of migration, exile, diaspora, cultural displacement.' (AN: 202) Unexpectedly, Bhabha's work explains these complex issues through the idea of the uncanny. The uncanny helps explain such issues because the migrant's uncanniness offers a lesson to us all. But if we are tempted to make the migrant experience the central experience of the modern world, we need to remember that not everyone moves around for the same reasons, and not everyone moves at all. Mass media theorist David Morley makes this point in his book *Home Territories*, reminding us of 'those vast realms of people who remain static, whether through choice or by force of circumstance'. (2000: 13–14) Movement around the world is accompanied by rootedness, and there is a delicately balanced relationship between the two that needs careful theorization.

With any theory, we need to be careful about its generalization, as Bhabha himself suggests in his commentary on Fanon and the dialectic. We have to attend to the specifics of each context or history. So, we cannot think about the whole of humanity as migrants, because this ignores the fact that so many people are not willing or able to move. The idea of the uncanny helps Bhabha think about the possibility that this last sector of humanity, forced into remaining static, has a relationship to home which is actually similar to the migrant's. Such a suggestion sounds like an absurdity, but it is meaningful as long as this similarity is not collapsed into sameness. For example, in *Uncanny Australia* (1998) Ken Gelder and Jane M. Jacobs discuss the aboriginal experience of the land. The land is both theirs and uncannily not theirs in the wake of European colonization: feted for having a special relationship with the land, at the same time they must contend with racist exclusion. In such an example, the uncanny helps us understand the experience of those who are bonded to the land, as well as those who restlessly move. In each case, the uncanny is a powerful description of the experience of the colonized.

For Bhabha, however, the uncanny has even more power when applied to the homeliness of the colonizer, when it is used to explore the foreignness necessarily central to the apparently original and self-sufficient source of colonization. Morley writes of 'the irreducible presence of alterity, in ourselves and in others' (2000: 265), and suggests that his book seeks 'a progressive notion of home, Heimat and community, which does not necessarily depend, for its effective functioning, on the exclusion of all forms of otherness, as inherently threatening to its own internally coherent self-identity'. (2000: 6) Such an identity is, of course, precisely the kind in which Bhabha is interested: 'home is a territory of both disorientation and relocation'. (HH: 12) Not every home is a castle, and through hospitality you gain as much as you lose, as I will now suggest.

'STRANGERS TO OURSELVES'

Many writers have drawn from Freud's understanding of the uncanny, but the writer most relevant to Bhabha's work is Julia Kristeva, specifically her book *Strangers to Ourselves*, which is an intervention into debates about immigration in France. One view of psychoanalysis sees it as inserting foreignness into the construct of reason, and Kristeva extends Freud's sense of a foreignness that is a necessary part of civilization:

Julia Kristeva (1941-) Kristeva is a Bulgarian psychoanalyst and philosopher who has worked in Paris since the 1960s. Although Gayatri Chakravorty Spivak has severely criticized the ethnocentrism of Kristeva's feminist vision (arguing that the book *About Chinese Women* (1977) is only about Chinese women insofar as they help western women deal with their own crises), postcolonial critics have found productive elements in her work. Kristeva's work is extremely varied, but Bhabha discusses two strands in particular. Her psychoanalytic writings on Freud have recently tended towards investigations of nationalism and immigration, emphasizing the foreignness that is always installed at the heart of the self, whether the individual or community (for example, *Strangers to Ourselves* (1991) and *Crisis of the European Subject* (2000)). Kristeva's psychoanalytic philosophy involves a critique of contemporary notions of European identity, and has practical implications in a time of European Union enlargement. It is an uncanny take on our identities. The second element of interest to Bhabha comes from her 'Women's Time', which elaborates *cyclical* and *monumental* time, associated with the maternal and repetition, distinguished from the time of history, *linear time*. Despite this separation, Kristeva acknowledges the practical and theoretical ways in which we should think about the two forms of time together.

> With Freud [...] foreignness, an uncanny one, creeps into the tranquility of reason itself, and, without being restricted to madness, beauty, or faith any more than to ethnicity or race, irrigates our speaking-being, estranged by other logics, including the heterogeneity of biology [...] Henceforth, we know that we are foreigners to ourselves, and it is with the help of that sole support that we can attempt to live with others. (Kristeva 1994: 170)

Even our bodies are foreign to us, according to Freud: they answer to biological drives, despite our attempts to repress these urges. Foreignness is not confined to any particular group, and the possibility of different groups living together depends on acceptance of this general truth.

So, Kristeva's book finds ethical principles in psychoanalysis; in doing this, she is following Freud, who always suggests that the clinical cure of the individual is relevant to the transformation of civilization in general. In other words, psychoanalysis might seem to be an individual form of cure, but its assumptions and procedures can help produce a more general, political position. The implications are clearly stated in Kristeva's book, in ways that coincide with Bhabha's thought. When we analyse a group identity like a nation, we are not trying to cure the nation of its ills, or trying to make the nation feel whole again. Instead, such analysis reveals that any nation is always in process, and so is always open to new cultural identities and forms. Only by emphasizing this open quality is it possible to maintain a fragile but real sense of coherent national identity. But we cannot equate coherence with being static. France, for example, should not try to assimilate new cultural forms into French culture, not least because French culture is not one thing itself: 'Psychoanalysis is [...] experienced as a journey into the strangeness of the other and of oneself, toward an ethics of respect for the irreconcilable. How could one tolerate a foreigner if one did not know one was a stranger to oneself?' (1994: 181–2) The important word here is *irreconcilable*: that we are all foreigners does not mean that we are all exactly the same. There can be no demand for assimilation into a culture: that we are all foreigners means that we cannot assign foreignness to other groups, and then dictate their actions or identities.

To put it another way, knowing how strange I am to myself helps me (at least) tolerate the strangeness of others, a strangeness that can be so easily viewed as threatening to my self identity. In fact, the relationship of self and other is an uncanny one. Kristeva describes an otherness that is always already within the self: she argues that all subjects are from the beginning haunted by uncanniness. But this feeling cannot be translated into a way of dividing the world between self and other: it does not allow us to divide foreigners, those who do not belong, from those who really do belong. Because psychoanalysis shows that we are all foreigners, even to ourselves, it becomes impossible to talk about foreigners at all. Such a perspective might sound abstractly philosophical, but Kristeva argues that it is political:

> The foreigner is within me, hence we are all foreigners. If I am a foreigner, there are no foreigners. Therefore Freud does not talk about them. The ethics of psychoanalysis implies a politics: it would involve a cosmopolitanism of a new sort that, cutting across governments, economies, and markets, might work for a mankind whose solidarity is founded on the consciousness of its unconscious – desiring, destructive, fearful, empty, impossible. (1994: 192)

To be a foreigner, in contrast to others, is obviously to be singled out, as asylum seekers around the world can testify. But if we are all foreigners, then it is possible to talk about a general quality of foreignness that defines all peoples. Such a general quality opens up the possibility of tolerance at least for those considered to be foreigners. That tolerant perspective cannot be the end of the story, but psychoanalysis is not a directly political discourse, and requires practical supplementation. Still, although there have been controversial debates concerning the general applicability of a practice as culturally specific as psychoanalysis, Kristeva's eloquent conviction is persuasive. But Bhabha would himself supplement her ideas. I suggested earlier that Kristeva is concerned about foreignness constitutive of any process of civilization. It will be clear from other chapters in this book that Bhabha cannot accept any equation of civilization and nation, and so might challenge her choice of terminology. None the less, particularly in its reference to cosmopolitanism, Kristeva's book fits Bhabha's concerns, not only in terms of the uncanny, but also minority rights, as I will explain in Chapter 7.

MAN AND HIS DOUBLES

Freud, Kristeva argues, denies that 'Man' is ever identical with himself. Each individual identity is split internally. But we can also think about 'Man' in wider terms, and look at our structures of knowledge about ourselves. This section explains how Bhabha develops ideas about the relatively recent nature of 'discourses of Man', meaning the human sciences like anthropology, sociology, and so on. Bhabha explores the ways that modernity's forms of knowledge are comparable to colonial knowledge. Remember the case of colonial knowledge, in which the colonized looks back at the colonizer, thereby unsettling his authority; similarly, colonialism uncannily returns to unsettle modernity. This uncanniness also marks a form of agency, reminding us of Bhabha's arguments about intersubjectivity, something central to his characterization of the colonial psychic economy. The post-colonial perspective is an uncanny one, and unsettles the self-definition of Western modernity, which has imagined itself to be separate from other cultural formations, or even unique (the 'clash of civilizations' thesis is evidence of such self-definition). Modernity is forced to confront its post-colonial doubles, after which it cannot stay the same.

In one suggestive example, the intellectual event known as the Second or Oriental Renaissance forced the West to confront its double, the East. The Italian Renaissance of the fifteenth century was viewed by German Romantic writers as incomplete or partial because of its overwhelming emphasis on rational enquiry; the qualities it lacked were provided by the Second Renaissance of the nineteenth century. In the Italian Renaissance, people were able to study Greek manuscripts that had become available after the fall of the Byzantine Empire. The Second Renaissance followed a similar pattern, European writers translating Sanskrit texts that became available with the decline of the Mogul Empire in India. In his book *The Oriental Renaissance*, orientalist scholar Raymond Schwab describes the following consequence of the Second Renaissance:

Asia has entered European thought like an invisible interlocutor [...] The second Renaissance challenged us as if it were juxtaposing us with another us,
forcing us to revise the known. An unknown seized us which, since it would
perhaps always have to remain unknown, became mysterious – mysterious
within every mind. Yes, here our horizons were opened and our wounds [...]
From then on would it not be the rational West that would be invited to justify itself? [...] It is difficult to localize, to identify. (Schwab 1984: 475–6)

In other words, the study of Sanskrit texts forced the West to
acknowledge the presence and force of another civilization, in a way
that the study of Greek texts had not. Instead of remaining self-sufficient in its identity, confident in its superiority, the West was forced
to reconsider its place in the world. Most importantly, rather than
concluding that Eastern civilization was completely other, the West
was actually unable to draw solid lines around itself. These texts
forced the recognition of similarity, and their doubling qualities
brought about an uncanny feeling, the sense that something long
denied was gradually making itself felt.

Chapter 6 explains how the nation is narrated in terms of pedagogy
and performance, the first being static, the second continually reintro-
ducing the effects of time, specifically the ongoing process of any identity becoming what it is, and therefore never being quite identical with
itself. Similarly, colonial authority is menaced by the colonized to the
extent that it utterly depends on the colonized for its sense of itself. It
is therefore not quite one with itself, and receives only uncertain con-
firmation of itself from 'the future'. In both these cases there is what
Bhabha calls a *time-lag*. Uncanniness is not only a question of place, but
also of time: because our sense of national identity is both static
(something we are taught) and open (something we are changing
through our everyday actions), we do not 'own' our nation. It is something that is simultaneously our own and not our own, because its
identity is always coming from the future or, in short, changing. The
same openness applies to a formation like modernity or post-
modernity. In Bhabha's 'The Postcolonial and the Postmodern', this
structure is re-elaborated in post-colonial terms, suggesting that the
post-colonial perspective demands that we alter our ideas about post-

modernity. Bhabha contends that post-modernity continues to be seen in sequential, historicist terms, as either a continuation of or a break from modernity.

To illustrate his point, he discusses Michel Foucault's *The Order of Things* (1970). This foundational post-structuralist text interrogates the 'discourse of Man' as a historical phenomenon rather than a natural way of ordering knowledge. Indeed, the heading of this section, 'Man and his Doubles', comes from Foucault's book. Foucault looks at how historical, anthropological, psychoanalytic, and other discourses came into being and ordered knowledge in a specific way, with the timeless figure of Man at their centre. *The Order of Things* suggests that we need to look again at 'our' ways of dividing, ordering, and de-limiting knowledge, which will allow us to see how culturally relative they are; accordingly, the book is an interesting complement to post-colonial criticism.

Importantly, Bhabha reads Foucault in terms of the uncanny, and the book itself invites this approach. For example, in the preface Foucault explains why he came to work on the project. He recalls reading a story by Argentinean writer Jorge Luis Borges (1899–1986). In the story there is an imaginary Chinese encyclopaedia that divides the world in a radically unfamiliar way (specifically animals, divided into categories like 'tame', 'fabulous', and 'that from a long way off look like flies'), at which Foucault simply laughs: he describes 'the laughter that shattered [...] all the familiar landmarks of my thought – *our* thought, the thought that bears the stamp of our age and our geography'. (1970: xvi) This laughter is occasioned by the invented encyclopaedia but not directed at it. Instead, Foucault is laughing at himself, if you like, or at least at the ways in which Western knowledge's universal pretensions might be so easily undermined. The book follows this insight to various conclusions about the potentially temporary nature of European discourses of Man.

However, Foucault surprisingly does not make any sustained reference to the fact of colonialism, and this absence lessens the impact of his analysis of Western knowledge. Despite this omission, Bhabha does not patiently correct Foucault, or supply the lack in his work, by producing a Foucault-inspired reading of colonialism. There is no need for such an undertaking, as Said's *Orientalism* already pursues that project. Instead, Bhabha suggests that the post-colonial perspective is already at work in Foucault's text. Importantly, as I have already mentioned, this perspective's workings are uncanny. For Bhabha, 'history confronts its uncanny doubles' (LC: 194) in Foucault, and 'the post-colonial perspective is subversively working in his text'. (LC: 195) Accordingly the connection between the discourse of Man and its unspoken colonial double can be explained in the following way:

> [T]he *heimlich* historical subject that arises in the nineteenth century cannot stop constituting the *unheimlich* knowledge of itself by compulsively relating one cultural episode to another in an infinitely repetitious series of events that are metonymic and indeterminate. The grand narratives of nineteenth-century historicism on which its claims to universalism were founded – evolutionism, utilitarianism, evangelism – were also, in another textual and territorial time/space, the technologies of colonial and imperialist governance. It is the 'rationalism' of these ideologies of progress that increasingly comes to be eroded in the encounter with the contingency of cultural difference. (LC: 195)

Like culture, Western knowledge is homely and unhomely, canny and uncanny. It is *both* abstractly idealistic *and* compromised by its application in real colonial contexts. One example is Mill's liberalism *at home and abroad*, to which Chapter 2 alluded: Mill was both liberal philosopher and colonial administrator, and colonial discourses operated both to claim moral and intellectual superiority, and to secure a practical domination. Similarly, the nineteenth century's advances in knowledge were at the same time functioning in colonial space – they were put into practice in 'other' places, far from the metropolis. Further, that practice quietly eroded the objective, rational character of such knowledge. Foucault elaborates how the supposed science of history is simultaneously followed to its logical conclusion in its uncanny, unscientific doubles – anthropology and psychoanalysis. It is not a significant leap to see how anthropology might constitute an uncanny irruption into the orders of Western knowledge, however much anthropology may seem to domesticate and quantify its objects of knowledge, i.e. 'other peoples'. In fact, as Chapter 6 explores, in the essay 'DissemiNation' Bhabha imagines an uncanny ethnography of the modern nation. What would this ethnography look like? One example is Caryl Phillips's travelogue *The European Tribe* (1987), in which he travels across 'a Europe I feel both of and not of'. (1987: xv) Phillips was born in St Kitts, and grew up in Britain; however, growing up black in the 1970s distanced him from fully identifying with Britain, and by extension with Europe. Such a dual perspective leads him to a searching examination of Europe as essentially *tribal*: his insights remain relevant in the twenty-first century, despite the superficial transformations of movement towards political integration. Of course in professional terms, as he himself points out, Phillips is a novelist rather than an anthropologist, but his book is clearly an uncanny ethnography.

As well as anthropology, the other uncanny double of history is psychoanalysis, which this chapter has discussed at length. Throughout his work, Bhabha uses psychoanalysis to conceptualize the relationship between modernity and its other, which we can call counter-modernity. The relationship he outlines is one of *transference*. In psychoanalysis, transference is the direction of desire towards a new object. Very often in the analytic situation the object is the analyst. Indeed, analysts are trained to avoid the opposite, counter-transference, as inimical to the analytic procedure. In Bhabha's use of the term, he is implying that the post-colonial perspective is that of the analyst, whilst Western modernity is the analysand (i.e. the subject being analysed). This is an extremely striking thought: post-colonial criticism is psychoanalysing Western modernity. This analysis finds that modernity has repressed its colonial origins, origins that install a foreignness within its identity from the very beginning. What is uncannily revealed, what might better have remained hidden from some perspectives, is that foreignness within the self.

Reading from the transferential perspective, where the Western ratio returns to itself from the time-lag of the colonial relation, then we see how modernity and postmodernity are themselves constituted from the marginal perspective of cultural difference. They encounter themselves contingently at the point at which the internal difference of their own society is reiterated in terms of the difference of the other, the alterity of the post-colonial site. (LC: 196)

Modernity seems to be coherent, but depends for its identity on a repressed and unspoken circuit running through different places and cultures. Those other cultures therefore are privileged places from which to observe modernity. This fact, despite being disavowed, is always breaking through into the conscious narratives of the West. Recall that Freud argues the uncanny was something obscurely familiar that yet should have remained hidden. That is what confronts Western modernity in the form of the post-colonial perspective. Bhabha implies that this perspective stands in place of the analyst in a general 'civilizational' analytic procedure, comparable to psychoanalytic treatment.

Of course, the fact is that psychoanalysis is necessarily a matter of *payment*, and it is impossible to claim that the colonized got paid, or even that the post-colonized received reparation. However, perhaps Bhabha's analogy can be taken too far, and his work does not extend the comparison further. In fact, this argument is a restatement of the position that the best testimony regarding modernity comes from counter-modernities that grew in colonized space:

> The dehistoricized authority of 'Man and his doubles' produces, in the same historical period, those forces of normalization and naturalization that create a modern Western disciplinary society. The invisible power that is invested in this dehistoricized figure of Man is gained at the cost of those 'others' – women, natives, the colonized, the indentured and enslaved – who, at the same time but in other spaces, were becoming the peoples without a history. (LC: 196–7)

Modernity's discourses floated free from their historical origins, at the same time as history was denied to modernity's others. In fact, the two are more than merely coincidental. Modernity's discourses deny historical depth to the colonized, in particular. They do this, as you will remember, in order to justify colonialism. The discourses of modernity are deeply implicated in the production of the colonial present. Accordingly, we cannot accept the terms of those discourses – at least not without serious qualification, or even complete transformation. A critical attitude to the colonial present requires something more than the simple repetition or application of those discourses. Post-modern critical discourses very often neglect the specific nature of the discourses to which they react. The important contribution of the uncanny science, psychoanalysis, is to remind us that a change of object requires a change, or at least a transformation, in the procedures of observation. Post-modern discourses provide that change, without explicitly facing the necessity for that change; post-colonial criticism makes the necessity explicit, reminding us that ways of knowing have long been complicit with structures of colonial domination.

'A PASSAGE TO INDIA'

The uncanny is necessarily a slippery concept, not least because it undermines the stability of concepts in general, which transforms their supposedly proper sense – and, you will remember from Chapter 2, transforming concepts is one of Bhabha's main theoretical strategies. This slippery quality means that it tends to elude definitive theorization. Accordingly, a specific example will clarify its explanatory power. Again, I have chosen a literary example, because of the origins of modern interest in the uncanny. In his writing, Freud explicitly brackets real-life uncanny experience, and pursues his object through literary examples. He suggests that uncanny real life experiences are not uncanny when represented in fiction, and also that literature produces many uncanny effects not achievable in real life. Bhabha, like many others, might feel that Freud has himself disallowed such a neat distinction between the literary and real life, but none the less literature has been a source of many intriguing examples of uncanniness, and continues to produce uncanny effects for post-colonial criticism (e.g. Punter 2000).

Accordingly, a literary example will help explain the post-colonial uncanny, and to conclude this chapter I will consider E. M. Forster's *A*

Passage to India, which becomes increasingly uncanny the more you read it, as you will begin to agree. The novel tells the story of Miss Quested, who travels from England to India to visit her fiancé, travelling with his mother Mrs Moore. The two are frustrated in their desires to see the 'real' India and Indians, as the local English have completely distanced themselves. The two are ultimately introduced to a doctor named Aziz, who takes them on a trip to the Marabar Hills. After the trip, Miss Quested accuses Aziz of rape. The rest of the novel explores the consequences of this accusation, and undermines the apparent polarization of England and India. Remembering what Bhabha has to say about probing the cunning (or *canniness*, I suggested) of modernity, read what runs through Mrs Moore's head as she listens to her son Ronny explaining the British mission in India:

> He spoke sincerely, but she could have wished with less gusto. How Ronny revelled in the drawbacks of his situation! How he did rub it in that he was not in India to behave pleasantly, and derived positive satisfaction therefrom! He reminded her of his public-schooldays. The traces of young-man humanitarianism had sloughed off, and he talked like an intelligent and embittered boy. His words without his voice might have impressed her, but when she heard the self-satisfied lilt of them, when she saw the mouth moving so complacently and competently beneath the little red nose, she felt, quite illogically, that this was not the last word on India. One touch of regret – not the canny substitute but the true regret from the heart – would have made him a different man, and the British Empire a different institution. (Forster 1924: 54)

Here the canniness in question is merely pretending to regret the brutalities of the colonial situation. However, this canniness has more general resonance in the novel, for example in the 'bridge party' supposedly designed to bridge the gap between ruler and ruled, but more likely to be a sharply polarized and deeply uncomfortable anti-social experience for everyone (and which is in sharp contrast to the *ad hoc* party at which Miss Quested and Mrs Moore are first invited by Aziz to the Marabar Hills). Despite its sympathies for individual characters, the novel usually seems to polarize the English and Indians in terms of canniness and uncanniness. This polarization can be seen in the following two passages. In the first, on the way to the Marabar Hills, the narrator takes a moment to reflect on the landscape, which is explicitly characterized in terms of uncanniness:

> There is something unspeakable in these outposts. They are like nothing else in the world, and a glimpse of them makes the breath catch. They rise abruptly, insanely, without the proportion that is kept by the wildest hills elsewhere, they bear no relation to anything dreamt or seen. To call them 'uncanny' suggests ghosts, and they are older than all spirit. Hinduism has scratched and plastered a few rocks, but the shrines are unfrequented, as if pilgrims, who generally seek the extraordinary, had here found too much of it. (1924: 130)

Later, to Fielding on his journey back to Europe, this supposed lack of proportion is all too clearly in contrast with the delights of the Mediterranean, as you will see below. The second passage I want to quote comes only a little later, once the party has left the train and is making its way by elephant to the caves themselves; it is a famous passage, but none the less is worth thinking about in relation to the novel's references to the uncanny:

> How can the mind take hold of such a country? Generations of invaders have tried, but they remain in exile. The important towns they build are only retreats, their quarrels the malaise of men who cannot find their way home. India knows of their trouble. She knows of the whole world's trouble, to its uttermost depth. She calls 'Come' through her hundred mouths, through objects ridiculous and august. But come to what? She has never defined. She is not a promise, only an appeal. (1924: 142)

This apparent emptiness, a projected centre or significance that is none the less absolutely inaccessible, is associated throughout the novel with India. For example, the echo that resounds throughout the latter half of the novel seems to be directly related to the uniquely dull, deadened echo of the caves; similarly, there is the never specified 'event' that befalls Miss Quested in the Marabar Caves. The novel apparently sets up an absolute division between canny Britain and uncanny India. A particularly clear example comes when Aziz tries to persuade Professor Godbole to explain to Miss Quested exactly what it is that is so unique about the caves. Aziz reflects that Godbole is not telling the whole story, that he is omitting the single most salient fact; Aziz then continues on to think about how his superior, Major Callendar, often accused him of doing the same thing. Aziz resolves to make an attempt to wrong-foot Godbole, to make him tell all, but never gets anywhere near discovering the truth: 'On he chattered, defeated at every move by an opponent who would not even admit that a move had been made, and further than ever from discovering what, if anything, was extraordinary about the Marabar Caves.' (1924: 80) Ultimately, Aziz never knows if there was any whole story to be told, just as the characters in the novel never really know if there was an event in the cave; of course, reading Forster's novel puts us in much the same position regarding an apparent gap never to be filled.

However, against this seemingly simple polarizing scheme, you might think about the strange connection between Mrs Moore and almost any Indian with whom she has contact, initially of course Aziz in the mosque; this connection productively blurs the clear-cut distinctions that sometimes, in a fairly programmatic way, mark Forster's novel. For example, think of the passage of Mrs Moore's ship, sadly now bereft of the woman herself as she has died not long after leaving India, as it moves into the Mediterranean: 'A ghost followed the ship up the Red Sea, but failed to enter the Mediterranean. Somewhere about Suez there is always a social change: the arrangements of Asia weaken and those of Europe begin to be felt, and during the transition Mrs Moore was shaken off.' (1924: 266) The Mediterranean does, indeed, become something of an unbreachable stronghold of European identity, however much such a construction might be questioned by the novel, as can be seen from Fielding's reflections as he reaches Venice (although, for him, Venice is not quite Europe anyway): 'The Mediterranean is the human norm. When men leave that exquisite lake, whether through the Bosphorus or the Pillars of Hercules, they approach the monstrous and extraordinary; and the southern exit leads to the strangest experience of all.' (1924: 293) Beyond Europe there is only *monstrosity*, but you will remember that doubling and the uncanny are frequently described in this way.

None the less, something of Mrs Moore's uncanny quality connects her with uncanny India, as indicated by Professor Godbole's strange *telepathic* sensations after the 'main event of the religious year' (1924: 302): 'He had, with increasing vividness, again seen Mrs. Moore, and round her faintly clinging forms of trouble. He was a Brahman, she Christian, but it made no difference, it made no difference whether she was a trick of his memory or a telepathic appeal.' (1924: 302–3) Telepathy, it should be said, was a source of fascination for Freud, yet another uncanny experience. Indeed, it is Aziz's encounter with Mrs Moore's equally uncanny son, Ralph, who seems to possess some strangely telepathic understanding of Aziz, which reminds us that for Forster the canny is just as likely to be found in India as in Britain. The novel undermines all simple divisions of domestic and foreign or proper and improper.

SUMMARY

In his constant questioning of oppositions, Bhabha makes use of various vocabularies. In the case of psychoanalysis he uses the idea of the uncanny, which has a wide contemporary critical currency, associated with monstrosity, repetition, and doubling. Bhabha uses both this term, and psychoanalysis more generally, to interrogate the superficial self-sufficiency of Western modernity's narratives. The uncanny, going back at least as far as Freud, makes any distinctions between the self and others problematic, and this consequence is explored and expanded by Kristeva's work. She makes the uncanny the basis of ethics, something that Bhabha extends further. Because colonial relationships have been on one level clearly relations between selves and others, anything that complicates the simple division of self and other is a powerful explanatory tool. The uncanny is a theme that recurs in Bhabha's work, but is also a mark of something his work is constantly doing – complicating simplistic oppositions.

The uncanny occurs when the originary or infantile is suddenly brought back into our consciousness, when we have our relationship to the present brought into question. On one level, colonialism lies back at the origins of Western modernity, and is therefore an aspect of its 'childhood'. This repressed fact returns uncannily in the contemporary moment. Bhabha explores this return in terms of the time-lag: colonialist self-understanding has detoured via the colonized and returned in the form of post-colonial anxiety and disjunction. Post-colonial readings of colonial literature, like Forster's novel, are not simple criticisms of the attitudes or ideas present in that literature, but instead aim to make the colonial return uncannily and therefore *usefully*. In the end, the category of the uncanny allows Bhabha to emphasize the connection between what troubles 'our' concepts and what troubles 'our' sense of self.

6

THE NATION

INTRODUCTION

The idea of the uncanny describes the dual quality of all identity, but is particularly useful in the study of colonialism. Bhabha uses the idea to complicate divisions between Western and non-Western identities, in other words large and abstract identities. But this complication also undermines the simple sense of identity claimed by real political forms, most obviously nations. Nations have been extremely important in discussions of colonialism, specifically forms of nationalism involved in anti-colonial struggle and post-colonial reconstruction. They have enabled stable cultural identities, as well as grounding necessary political structures: oppressed peoples have identified with clear national identities. Therefore, nations have seemed a vital organizing principle for many writers in post-colonial studies (for example Ahmad 1992). However, Bhabha rejects the well-defined and stable identity associated with the national form. It is not that he rejects national identity entirely, but that he wants to keep such identity open. He achieves this by examining the 'narration' of nations; indeed, he edited a collection called *Nation and Narration*. Nations have their own narratives, but very often a dominant or official narrative overpowers all other stories, including those of minority groups. Such minority or marginalized groups have privileged perspectives on the rethinking of national identities, helping to make them more inclusive and realistic.

One way to think about the narration of nations is to see how public figures exemplify or challenge national identity. For example, in an article from the journal *Artforum*, Bhabha writes about Diana, Princess of Wales. In this article, 'Designer Creations', he explains Diana's appeal in the following way:

> Her affiliative community, in the realms of public concern and communication, was not limited to the victims of social inequity traditionally contained within the platform and prerogative of national politics – the unemployed, the working classes. Her concern for AIDS victims, and those who were threatened, life and limb, by the presence of landmines, gave her an international demesne and a cosmopolitan appeal that the royal family had stoutly resisted. (DC: 14)

In short, Diana became much more than British. Indeed, the figure of Diana suggests a way of narrating nationality distinct from that commonly associated with royalty. She opens one national narrative focused around the monarchy to genuinely *inter*national connections. Monarchy may once have been central to the British Empire, but that form of international narration was very much between clearly delineated nations. Diana's international appeal transcends nationality. In fact, elsewhere Diana is seen as one instance of the way that philanthropic individuals (like financier George Soros or Microsoft's Bill Gates) have become examples of 'world citizenship' (CM: 581), even if that fact demonstrates the current limitations of that citizenship. In any case, the response to Diana's death in the UK (and elsewhere) perhaps indicates an appropriately *trans*national spirit. We could argue about the exact extent to which she caught a mood, or created that mood, but what is clear is that she had some sense of the importance of media presentation, a sense often still lacking in the family into which she married. She understood the media invention of identity and nationality. Diana's role in various national narratives might be read as symptomatic. Something in the reaction to her death, then, might optimistically be taken as sign of changed national consciousness. That change is something that is difficult to come to terms with, and should not be equated with discussion of a 'Britain that is not afraid to cry'. Such a change, however, is for Bhabha much less to do with the content of the consciousness than its form. To explain why changing the form of national narratives is important, this chapter will elaborate Bhabha's understanding of nation and community, initially by looking at literary and cinematic narratives, and later by thinking about pedagogy – teaching.

'YOUNG SOUL REBELS'

That nations have narratives is not really a startling thought. Histories are, after all, narratives, and perhaps school history often focuses on national history. When we think of national histories it is, of course, tempting to think in terms of periods, particularly those associated with individuals: 'The Reagan Years', for example. This practice might seem rather natural, but has also been criticized for being artificial. One way of looking at musical history, for example, would see the 1970s as some hideous aberration after the magic of the 1960s, but the world of music did not collapse when The Beatles split. In other words, pivotal dates have a habit of making us see discontinuities when really there are also many continuities. None the less, it is probably not too misleading to think of some dates as particularly important, even if there is no specific dramatic historical event to which we are attaching importance. In the UK context, one of these dates is 1977, the year of the Queen's Silver Jubilee, so what I am about to say is immediately linked back to what Bhabha proposes about Diana. Talking in *Sight and Sound*, Bhabha and sociologists Paul Gilroy and Stuart Hall discuss British director Isaac Julien's film *Young Soul Rebels* (1991). The film is set during the week of the Silver Jubilee, when two DJs in London's East End become involved in a tale of murder, racist confrontation, and the eventual triumph of a hybrid musical culture. The film's thriller plot is perhaps less interesting than the convergence of themes and musical forms, bringing together usually overlooked aspects of the period, and perhaps even *inventing* a 1977 that is relevant to the 1990s. Julien, it can be argued, kick-starts the circulation of ideas and identities that have become so stable when we think of 1977. This circulation is what interests Bhabha, who says the following about the film:

> The 1977 Silver Jubilee was so much about the celebration of local commu-
> nity, with all those 'little Englands' decked out in red, white and blue bunting.
> The film turns this on its head and shows that there exists a range of cultural
> localities that conflict or coexist with each other. That's what makes a tran-
> sient, transitional youth culture such an excellent choice for a film about sex-
> uality and ethnicity – it doesn't allow either of these identities to become
> fixed. (TP: 18)

Stereotypical images of the UK in 1977 can focus on two related stories – that of the Jubilee and that of the Sex Pistols, particularly 'God Save the Queen'. Both narratives have produced stable identities, opposed now just as they were then. Even the Sex Pistols' anti-establishment single, surreptitiously denied its place at the top of the charts, has assumed its place in the fixed story of that year. Julien's film converts 1977 into a very different kind of pivotal date, placing emphasis on cultural and social phenomena marginalized in many histories – sexuality and funk. Julien and cultural critic Kobena Mercer write that, when central and marginal identities come together in this way, the conjuncture 'speaks of – articulates – conflicting identities within the "imagined community" of the nation'. (Deitcher 2000) We are reminded of the heterogeneity of any national identity. In *Young Soul Rebels*, identities connected to ethnicity and sexuality are foregrounded, but importantly for Bhabha they are not monumentalized as absolute alternatives to the narratives of the Jubilee year. These identities are not naturalized. Bhabha suggests instead that these identities derive from creative and agonistic processes, and are therefore in ongoing and open relation with temporality. They don't just transpire, finally and forever, after a period of necessary struggle. Bhabha goes on to suggest that 'Community has to be created and negotiated; it isn't just there because you are black or gay.' (TP: 19)

If this is true of any communal identity, or any identity whatsoever, then we need to pay particular attention to why Bhabha thinks this instance is important. In the longer quotation he emphasizes the transience and transitional nature of the culture portrayed in the film. It is not necessarily that he feels there is something more impermanent about punk, 'Rock Against Racism', and other subcultural phenomena from that time. Instead, these sub-cultural phenomena simply have less interest in aligning themselves with naturalized, permanent, or 'traditional' values. Accordingly, this is an excellent place to look at the negotiation of identities simply because there is little or no resistance to this negotiation. In fact, this negotiation is almost a theme of the film. Moreover, it is something that exceeds simple thematic presentation: rather than simply theorizing it, this negotiation comes through in Julien's combination of sound and image. The imagination of national identity is a matter of both form and content.

IMAGINING THE NATION

Bhabha, like many other thinkers, takes Benedict Anderson's book *Imagined Communities* (1991) as a starting point to think about nations. Perhaps the title will seem straightforward enough, with that word 'imagination' perhaps a little too easily bisected: imagi-nation. However, it is important to remember that imagined things are not imaginary or unreal, at least not in the sense that we could dismiss them from our thinking. You could argue that imagined communities are simultaneously real and unreal, ghostly or virtual. Although it is possible to think increasingly in terms of virtual communities enabled by new technologies, communities surpassing or exceeding the nation, Anderson's book reminds us that the nation itself has always been a virtual community. This is true in several senses. First, he suggests that, although the nation-state is historically specific and relatively recent, nations themselves always have an air of ahistorical permanence: 'If nation-states are widely conceded to be "new" and "historical," the nations to which they give political expression always loom out of an immemorial past, and, still more important, glide into a limitless future.' (1991: 11–12) Nations, in other words, are forms of mythology. Bhabha rephrases this thought to emphasize the connection between nation and narration: 'Nations, like narratives, lose their origins in the myths of time and only fully realize their horizons in the mind's eye.' (NN: 1)

None the less, right now the nation will always seem to be at one with itself. The second virtual quality of the nation stresses this coincidence of the nation with itself. Anderson suggests that the modern nation is a matter of simultaneity, with each member of the imagined community precisely able to imagine him- or herself as one among many, right here, right now. This simultaneity is horizontal, in contrast to the non-rational, divine simultaneity of monarchical structures preceding the modern nation. It is largely enabled by the advent of modern print languages, and given expression by novels and newspapers: the novel form has long been connected to the rise of modern European nations, its structures analogous to the imagination of the nation, and the newspaper clearly has a literal simultaneity, with millions of people in any nation reading the same stories in the same language, on the same day and at the same time. Anderson suggests that this *calendrical* element of the nation is important: 'The idea of a sociological organism moving calendrically through homogeneous, empty time is a precise analogue of the idea of the nation, which is also conceived as a solid community moving steadily down (or up) history.' (1991: 26) The phrase 'homogeneous, empty time' alludes to the work of German critic Walter Benjamin (1892–1940), and suggests that the passage of the nation through history is, even in time of war, serene and unimpeded by disjunction or dislocation. Nations seem to be self-identical, confident in their historical destiny even under duress – perhaps duress makes the nation even *more* itself, inspiring the 'Blitz spirit', for example. In other words, even in the most testing historical moment, the nation hangs together, utterly simultaneous, and at one with itself. It is to this notion that Bhabha, like many others, has turned his attention. His work is constantly seeking to undermine the complacent and pernicious insistence on a simultaneity that tends, of course, to exclude those that do not fit.

PERFORMING THE NATION

If you read Salman Rushdie's novel *The Moor's Last Sigh* (1996) after reading Homi Bhabha, you might experience a moment of uncanny recognition. The narrator's mother is an artist, Aurora Zogoiby, who paints in a variety of styles on which her son comments. For one exhibition catalogue in particular, a comedic art historian called Dr Vakil contributes a strikingly titled essay, 'Imperso-Nation and Dis/Semi/Nation: Dialogics of Eclecticism and Interrogations of Authenticity in A.Z.' The Bhabha essay that I am about to discuss bears the not dissimilar title 'DissemiNation: Time, narrative and the margins of the modern nation'. The similarity is not to Bhabha's discredit, because Rushdie's novel offers various expressions of a hybrid space very much in the Bhabha idiom. For example, Aurora offers this striking vision of identity:

> Place where worlds collide, flow in and out of one another, and washofy away. Place where an air-man can drowno in water, or else grow gills; where a water-creature can get drunk, but also chokeofy, on air. One universe, one dimension, one country, one dream, bumpo'ing into another, or being under, or on top of. Call it Palimpstine. (Rushdie 1996: 226)

This passage, despite the novel's many strange pastiche passages of art history and film theory, appears to be a straightforward and serious expression of history and identity, as forms of *palimpsest*. Palimpsests are overwritten, heavily annotated manuscripts, on which earlier writing is still visible underneath newer writing: they offer a suggestive model of hybrid identity. The passage from Rushdie is not quite so easily explained, however, and all those universes competing for space, forcing themselves between and into one another, unavoidably call up Bhabha's sense of the nation, here not only the Western nation but India too. Rushdie's novel expresses many of the anxieties to which such a palimpsestical perspective might contribute, and to which Aurora herself falls victim. For example, Abraham's ancestors are traced back to Boabdil the Moor, something which in practice irritates Aurora. The narrator rhetorically asks, '*My mother who insists on the purity of our race, what say you to your forefather the Moor?*' (1996: 82)

More importantly still, Rushdie implies connections that Bhabha makes explicit in his essay, concerning the identical and the non-identical, the static and the processual. The narrator portrays his mother as a confused secular resident of Mumbai in the second half of the twentieth century: 'It was easy for an artist to lose her identity at a time when so many thinkers believed that the poignancy and passion of the country's immense life could only be represented by a kind of selfless, dedicated – even patriotic – mimesis.' (1996: 173) As Bhabha will argue, it is vital for the artist, on the side of what he calls the *performative*, to resist the easy temptations of the static and the self-sameness of community, that is, the *pedagogical*.

What does Bhabha mean by these two terms? The essay gives definitions, and after explaining the definitions I will go into detail about its general statements, as they help cross-reference these notions with his arguments about colonial authority. The definitions help us understand how ambivalence is not just a question of colonial authority, but also post-colonial nationality, and that this ambivalence is a question of temporality: 'The language of culture and community is poised on the fissures of the present becoming the rhetorical figures of a national past.' (LC: 142) Bhabha refers to 'the disjunctive time of the nation's modernity'; we are, he suggests, caught 'between the shreds and patches of cultural signification and the certainties of a nationalist pedagogy'. (LC: 142) On the one hand, we have 'the continuist, accumulative temporality of the pedagogical', and on the other, there is 'the repetitious, recursive strategy of the performative'. (LC: 145) The pedagogical and performative always, necessarily, go together, but how do they work? Bhabha suggests that the whole idea of 'the people' emerges from 'a double narrative movement'. (LC: 145) The people, like the nation, are a strategy: a *rhetorical* strategy. This double movement is that of pedagogy and performance, of certainties and anxieties, which always go together. Bhabha's explanation of the double movement, and its strange temporality, is the following:

> We then have a contested conceptual territory where the nation's people must be thought in double-time; the people are the historical 'objects' of a nationalist pedagogy, giving the discourse an authority that is based on the

pre-given or constituted historical origin *in the past*; the people are also the 'subjects' of a process of signification that must erase any prior or originary presence of the nation-people to demonstrate the prodigious, living principles of the people as contemporaneity: as that sign of the *present* through which national life is redeemed and iterated as a reproductive process. (LC: 145)

This doubling, analogous to so many other repetitions in Bhabha's work, cannot be a re-iteration of the nation as a clearly defined identity. Rather, as is implied by the explanation of 'iteration' in Chapter 2, re-iteration always brings with it the strange, uncanny sense that what is being re-iterated was never fully there itself. There is never any 'itself' to be repeated. As Bhabha writes in 'Articulating the Archaic', 'the repetition of the "same" can in fact be its own displacement'. (LC: 137) On the one hand, pedagogy tells us that the nation and the people are what they are; on the other, performativity keeps reminding us that the nation and the people are always generating a non-identical excess over and above what we thought they were. It might be argued that even the pedagogical is caught up in this logic of the performative. The apparent stability of pedagogical statements is actually caught by the need to endlessly re-state the reality of a nation constantly exceeding its definition. If the pedagogical is caught up in the performative in this way, then the consequence is a familiar blurring of apparently polarized categories, so that although I have defined the two, and have quoted Bhabha defining the two, it is not easy to divide and define them. Bhabha writes that 'In place of the polarity of a pre-figurative self-generating nation "in-itself" and extrinsic to other nations, the performative introduces a temporality of the "in-between".' (LC: 148) In the same way, the polarity of pedagogical and performative is constantly blurring, so that the pedagogical is never as stable as it wants to be, and the performative itself becomes pedagogically important.

BEING THE NATION

Bhabha makes the following claim: 'The nation fills the void left in the uprooting of communities and kin, and turns that loss into the

language of metaphor.' (LC: 139) Earlier chapters have already indicated that Bhabha's sympathies are more usually with metonymy.
Metaphor appears to imply some reality, some origin, back there, to
which we might return; in terms of a linear, *horizontal*, historicist narrative, the nation stands for a secure, if nostalgic, vision of community.
However, for Bhabha, 'the space of the modern nation-people is never
simply horizontal'. (LC: 141) Many critics of Bhabha have objected to
his perceived dismissal of nationalism, pointing out that actually existing forms of anti-colonialism have drawn strength from various forms
of nationalism. However, here he insists that he is not really interested
in nationalism. Nationalism is on the side of metaphor, of attempted
stabilization and horizontality, rather than metonymy's ambivalent vertical shifts without stable conclusion. Already he makes clear that the
focus of his essay will be temporality, a certain attitude to time that
resists historicism. This emphasis will again be familiar, if you recall the
passages in earlier chapters explaining the connections between realism, historicism, and colonial authority. 'DissemiNation' essentially
argues that nations do not have to be conceived in historicist terms,
and this is the central point to grasp because for Bhabha nations are
forms of narration:

> The linear equivalence of event and idea that historicism proposes, most
> commonly signifies a people, a nation, or a national culture as an empirical
> sociological category or a holistic cultural entity. However, the narrative and
> psychological force that nationness brings to bear on cultural production
> and political projection is the effect of the ambivalence of the 'nation' as a
> narrative strategy. As an apparatus of symbolic power, it produces a contin-
> ual slippage of categories, like sexuality, class affiliation, territorial paranoia,
> or 'cultural difference' in the act of writing the nation. What is displayed in
> this displacement and repetition of terms is the nation as the measure of the
> liminality of cultural modernity. (LC: 140)

Like colonial authority, the power of a national narrative seems
entirely confident of its consistency and coherence, but is all the while
undermined by its inability to really fix the identity of the people,
which would be to limit their identity to a single overpowering nation-

ality. The narrative of nationality is continually displaced by other identities, like sexuality, class, or race, and there can be no end to this displacement. Indeed, we should not desire any such end, because that would be to accept a fixed and therefore stereotypical idea of any national identity. This familiar double structure is, I have just said, the same structure found in colonial authority, and is the doubling so well captured by the idea of the uncanny. Importantly, however, in the last sentence of the above passage Bhabha sees the nation as the most important *symptom* in an ethnographic study of modernity: again, this suggests the idea that post-colonial criticism is a psychoanalysis of modernity, with the nation as a privileged example.

This privileged example reminds us that, when we change the object of study, we need also to change the method of study. This change is implied by the logical structures that are being analysed: the play between the pedagogical and the performative means that category of 'the people' constitutes both an established fact and an open becoming. 'We' are made to be both the speaker and the spoken of, the *spoken-into-being*, and so 'the position of narrative control is neither monocular nor monologic'. (LC: 150) Bhabha refers to the influential structuralist anthropologist Claude Lévi-Strauss's characterization of the ethnographic act, in which the observer must simultaneously be part of the observed. For a long time European ethnography was the study of other peoples in other places. By contrast, when Bhabha sees the nation as a symptom in the ethnography of modernity, this ethnography is turned within, onto the apparently self-same, stable identity of the West: 'It becomes a question of otherness of the people-as-one. The national subject splits in the ethnographic perspective of culture's contemporaneity and provides both a theoretical position and a narrative authority for marginal voices or minority discourse.' (LC: 150) If the aim is to unsettle the West's sense of itself, then historical accident privileges the minoritarian perspective, to which I will now turn.

PERSPECTIVES ON NATIONHOOD

The implications of the doubled time of the nation need to be clarified, because we seem to be in much the same position as we were regarding colonial authority, which you will remember is also a matter of ambivalence. This understanding of the nation is superficially appealing, but is this ambivalence or anxiety merely confined to the apparently unified nation, and if it is not, what difference does it actually make? The pedagogical seems to be a reifying, deadening figuration of the nation, and its acknowledgement at best a recognition of the problems if not anxieties of official narratives. However, the anxiety in question is of course not confined to the official versions of the nation, and in fact is elsewhere felt not as anxiety but as opportunity; Bhabha writes that 'Minority discourse acknowledges the status of national culture – and the people – as a contentious, performative space of the perplexity of the living in the midst of the pedagogical representations of the fullness of life.' (LC: 157) Rather than trying to wish away the contingent, processual nature of identity's becoming, minority cultures embrace the disjunctive temporal relation.

One of Bhabha's examples (developed at length in 'How Newness Enters the World') is Salman Rushdie's *The Satanic Verses*, and it is this novel I will explore in more detail to explain how the minority or migrant perspective comes to rewrite narratives of nationality. In this case, whatever the controversies around the novel might suggest, it is the narratives of Englishness that are revised and rewritten. *The Satanic Verses* is an extremely difficult novel to introduce, due to its wealth of stories and styles, but the anchoring narrative tells the story of Gibreel Farishta, movie legend, and Saladin Chamcha, who at the beginning of the novel fall from a destroyed jet towards the sea, singing competing verses in an ongoing contest between good and evil. The other main plot of the novel is 'dreamed' by Gibreel, and tells the story of Mahound, based on the seventh-century foundation of Islam. Bhabha sees the novel's multiple narratives, and the real-life events surrounding it, as evidence of the precariousness of in-between, hybrid identities. Writing in *Artforum* about the novel and its reception, Bhabha comments:

> What the book uniquely reveals is a life lived precariously on the cultural and political margins of modern society. Where once we could believe in the comforts and continuities of tradition, today we must face the responsibilities

of cultural translation. In the attempt to mediate between different cultures, languages, and societies, there is always the threat of mistranslation, confusion, and fear. (ATL: 12)

Hybridity is not something simply to be celebrated, in a magical multiculturalist re-invention of tired national traditions, but is a difficult, agonistic process of negotiation, as Rushdie experienced. In fact, this example will emphasize the extent to which Bhabha does not simply celebrate hybridity. In his essay 'In Good Faith', written in the aftermath of the controversy surrounding the novel (following its publication, the book was banned by various countries, and Rushdie was placed under a death sentence by Iranian leader Ayatollah Ruhollah Khomeini), Rushdie writes of his wish to celebrate 'hybridity, impurity, intermingling, the transformation that comes of new and unexpected combinations of human beings, cultures, ideas politics, movies, songs'. (1992: 394) Of course, the controversy itself reminds us that, in sociologist Paul Gilroy's words, 'occupying the space between [identities] or trying to demonstrate their continuity has been viewed as a provocative and even oppositional act of political insubordination'. (1993: 1)

Gilroy's sense of the political is broader than party politics, and his comment is an appropriate characterization of the form of insubordination performed by and thematized in *The Satanic Verses*. The novel is an assault on what Rushdie calls 'the absolutism of the Pure'. (1992: 394) Its enigmatic narrative voice mocks, subverts, and destroys the many fictions of pure identity that the main characters Gibreel and Saladin encounter, and this is of course just as true if not more so in the case of supposedly secular Britain as it is of India and in particular, as many too easily think they know, one version of Islam. The novel's narrative models, drawn from Indian traditions, modernism, and postmodernism, have an extremely disorienting effect, and the very last thing they might be reduced to is a historicist vision of homogeneous, empty time. The narrative traditions clearly embrace multiplicity, with characters and stories flowing into one another; there is also the recurring motif of blurring dreams and reality, most vividly expressed by Saladin's entrance, in his transformed state, into the popular imagination: 'What was happening, although nobody admitted it or even, at first, understood, was that everyone, black brown white, had started thinking of the dream figure as *real*, as a being who had crossed the frontier.' (Rushdie 1988: 288) Frontiers are there to be crossed, at least if they are fictional rather than legal or political.

Likewise, the novel's juxtaposition of stories is not as stark as it initially seems, and one way of reading its sections on Mahound and Jahilia is to see them as expressions of Gibreel's anxiety over his identity. Gibreel's incredulity as the prophet leaves their meetings with someone else's words in his ears is a measure of his own lack of control over his identity. Gibreel is a film star, and accordingly questions of identity become particularly complex here with the supposed division between public and private. None the less, the contrast between Gibreel at the beginning and the end of the novel suggests that his restlessness and his desire to reinvent his identity, coupled with his inability to do so in any final sense, lead to his suicide. At the novel's start Gibreel sings a song to Saladin that is suggestive in the light of his death: ' "To be born again," sang Gibreel Farishta tumbling from the heavens, "first you have to die." ' (1988: 3) Finally, he kills himself, 'and was free', but what he is free from is obscure. Despite his personal performance of identity, Gibreel remains attached to an impossible pedagogical certainty. Certainly, the remains of an identity that he continually attempted to lose are finally shaken off, but perhaps along with *all* semblance of identity. At one point we read the following characterization of Gibreel, alongside Saladin:

> Gibreel, for all his stage-name and performances, and in spite of born-again slogans, new beginnings, metamorphoses; – has wished to remain, to a large degree, *continuous* – that is, joined to and arising from the past. [...] whereas Saladin Chamcha is a creature of *selected* discontinuities, a *willing* re-invention. (1988: 427)

The lesson (and programmatic passages like the one above indicate that this really is a lesson) of Gibreel is that identity cannot be approached in the rigid, uncompromising way that he adopts. By contrast, Saladin's ultimate happiness is founded on a more fluid conception of identity, a conception made ironic by some of his own attitudes. Throughout, Zeeny casts him as a reactionary apologist for colonialism; when Mishal and Anahita declare themselves to be British, Saladin thinks otherwise: 'But they weren't British, he wanted to tell them: not *really*, not in any way he could recognise. And yet his old certainties were slipping away by the moment, along with his old life.' (1988: 259) This last sentence is of course important, because it is precisely through this loss of his old certainties that Saladin is saved. When his body is transformed into the devil's, he is comforted by Sufyan in what is both a comic moment and one of the novel's central passages. Sufyan refers Saladin to the wisdom of the classical age, in particular to Lucretius and Ovid:

> 'For me it is always Ovid over Lucretius,' [Sufyan] said. 'Your soul, my good poor dear sir, is the same. Only in its migration it has adopted this presently varying form.'
>
> 'This is pretty cold comfort,' Chamcha managed a trace of his old dryness. 'Either I accept Lucretius and conclude that some demonic and irreversible mutation is taking place in my most inmost depths, or I go with Ovid and concede that everything now emerging is no more than a manifestation of what was already there.' (1988: 277)

Although Rushdie's novels apparently always celebrate and exemplify the Ovidian perspective, like Saladin they yet make room for the nominally opposing view, meaning that the notion of a glorious multicultural hybridity is always slightly undermined, and always therefore a little anxious. It is always just possible that the wondrous hybrid will be caught between two (or more) monolithic identities. Alternatively, there is the possibility that the migrant will learn the lessons of the pedagogical nation all too well, something about which the Imam warns Bilal X, singer turned voice-of-the-revolution: 'to be raised in the house of power is to learn its ways, to soak them up, through that very skin that is the cause of your oppression'. (1988: 211) Perhaps unsurprisingly, Rushdie has been criticized for providing an orientalist perspective on Islam, in the way Said describes in *Orientalism*.

None the less, *The Satanic Verses* gives at least as searching a representation of Britain as it does of Islam. Rushdie's Britain is a secular society followed to a logical conclusion, and with predictable problems. But it is not only Britain that has gone wrong, as he writes in *Imaginary Homelands*: 'India has arrived at a full-blown crisis of descriptions.' (1992: 2) If this crisis is a crisis of the pedagogical, then we might read Rushdie's work as the forceful expression of the performative or poetic element of national narration. Towards the close of the novel, we read the following passage: ' "These days," [Swatilkeha] insisted, "our positions must be stated with crystal clarity. All metaphors are capable of misinterpretation." ' (1988: 537) However, such a sentiment goes entirely against the force of the novel, and it is not surprising that Swatilkeha quickly retracts the proposition. Metaphors may still give the illusion of stability, but this is in many ways a novel of boundless metonymy.

The novel's celebration of hybridity is given a conclusive expression in the person of Saladin Chamcha, whose surprising realization of his potential comes as he watches a TV gardening programme:

> There it palpably was, a chimera with roots, firmly planted in and growing vigorously out of a piece of English earth: a tree, he thought, capable of taking the metaphoric place of the one his father had chopped down in a distant garden in another, incompatible world. If such a tree were possible, then so was he; he, too, could cohere, send down roots, survive. Amid all the televisual images of hybrid tragedies [...] he was given this one gift. It was enough. He switched off the set. (1988: 406)

The tree conjures up many traditional figures of place and identity, but of course Rushdie does not handle the question of roots in a straightforward manner. The tree emphasizes the fact that India is precisely not an 'incompatible' world, even if transition or translation between Britain and India is problematic and provisional. The image of the tree recurs in the novel, in the context of the re-imagination of British society, and it is here that this chapter will return to Bhabha's writing. The migrant is both the gardener and the garden, and so is both the speaker and the spoken-into-being. As Dr Simba's mother suggests in her speech at the public meeting: 'We have been made again: but I say that we shall also be the ones to remake this society, to shape it from the bottom to the top. We shall be the hewers of the dead wood and the gardeners of the new.' (1988: 414) We have been made, and we shall be the makers: such a formulation provides a brief encapsulation of the doubled time of the migrant, of which *The Satanic Verses* is exemplary.

COMMUNITY AND NATION

It is important to state that, just because Bhabha seems to place all emphasis on the performative at the expense of the pedagogical, it does not mean he thinks we can dispense completely with the static, or indeed totality and the holistic; such things will be transformed, however. So, 'DissemiNation' superficially seems to imply a dismissal of the usefulness of the nation as a category and as a political structure; it also seems to devalue notions of community in their most familiar forms. *Nation* and *community* remain important, it is just that they need to be imagined in new ways. We might want to place these terms in quotation marks, to remind us that we should be careful how we use them. None the less, there are positive revisions that we might make to them. For example, if you look at the original text of 'DissemiNation', you will see that the passage quoted earlier concerning minority discourse's seizure of the performative is followed by this significant qualification: 'Now there is no reason to believe that such marks of difference cannot inscribe a "history" of the people or become the gathering points of political solidarity.' (LC: 157) Further, post-colonial and feminist temporalities, Bhabha writes, 'challenge us to think the question of community and communication *without* the moment of transcendence'. (LC: 153) Speaking in 1991, Bhabha says the following about the nation:

> I don't think we can eliminate the concept of the nation altogether, at a time when in many parts of the world – in South Africa, in Eastern Europe – people are actually living and dying for that form of society. You can't completely do away with the nation as an idea or as a political structure, but you *can* acknowledge its historical limitations for our time. (ANI: 82)

However, any rethinking of these categories must be thorough going. Remember that Bhabha's logic of hybridity does not in any way coincide with 'official' versions of multiculturalism, as he indicates in 'DissemiNation' when he writes that 'Cultural difference must not be understood as the free play of polarities and pluralities in the homogeneous empty time of the nation community.' (LC: 162) For Bhabha there is little to be gained through licensing a change in national content without a corresponding change in national form, for the latter will always constrain and even undermine the former. The serene, gliding form of the total sociological organism, as described by Benedict Anderson (1991), must be forcefully reminded of its self-divisions.

NATION AND EDUCATION

One issue suggested by Bhabha's reference to the pedagogical is the connection between English studies and national narratives. Matthew Arnold (1822–1888), poet and inspector of schools in Victorian Britain, consciously conceived a social function for literary study, designed to promote class solidarity and produce 'civilized' colonial administrators. Various critics have investigated how English studies produced a certain sense of national identity, either at home or throughout the British empire (Baldick 1983; Viswanathan 1989). Accordingly, Bhabha's rethinking of the narration of nations invites us to remake education, particularly perhaps English studies, to accord with the realities of hybridity rather than idealized projections of coherence. His sense of the need to re-invent Britain (see RB) begins with the need to communicate innovations in art and cultural theory to other practitioners, some of whom will write school curricula and teach in the classroom – Bhabha's ideas ought to have practical use in transforming education.

Such a revision of educational policy, curricula, and so on, might seem one of the aims of multiculturalism, and has certainly been widely discussed for many years in Britain (devolution is obviously important here also). The controversial Parekh Report on *The Future of Multi-Ethnic Britain*, published by the Runnymede Trust in 2000, is explicit on the continued need for such an educational revision; in a chapter with the suggestive title 'Rethinking the National Story', the following passage discusses 'the end of empire':

> This is often described as the shedding of a burden whose time has passed. However, expunging the traces of an imperial mentality from the national culture, particularly those that involved seeing the white British as a superior race, is a much more difficult task. This mentality penetrated everyday life, popular culture and consciousness. It remains active in projected fantasies and fears about difference, and in racialized stereotypes of otherness. The unstated assumption remains that Britishness and whiteness go together, like roast beef and Yorkshire pudding. There has been no collective working through of this imperial experience. The absence from the national curriculum of a rewritten history of Britain as an imperial force, involving dominance in Ireland as well as Africa, the Caribbean and Asia, is proving from this perspective to be an unmitigated disaster. (2000: 24–5)

A crucial point suggested by this chapter is that the history taught in schools narrates a nation, with all the implications that might follow from omissions, hesitations, and controversial viewpoints (it should also be remembered that the educational systems of England, Northern Ireland, Scotland, and Wales are not identical). For example, as the Parekh Report suggests, the British Empire seems to have been systematically excluded from the national curriculum, and this has led to widespread debate, with people of differing political sympathies arguing strongly that study of empire needs to be reinstated. Simple reinstatement of historical facts, however, could not be enough from Bhabha's perspective, although it is obviously good to stop pretending certain histories did not happen. Britain needs to be performed as what it is: a hybrid nation. It cannot be merely taught as such, as if it were a pre-existent bounded phenomenon, for that would still entail a static approach and would imply the possibility of keeping things as they are right now, a possibility provoking strong feelings.

Such feelings would seem to be what we see in virulent reactions to the issue of asylum. Indeed, the dangers of official multiculturalism, with its vision of pre-existent cultures meeting in bounded national space, are everywhere apparent, as Chapter 7 will suggest. For example, critic Gargi Bhattacharyya writes the following about cultural education in Britain:

> Government sponsorship of 'multiculturalism' appears [...] as an attempt to concoct a non-ethnocentric schooling in nationhood. If this is the case, critics of racial injustice must develop more sophisticated arguments than the demand for representation of diversity in cultural education. The operation of a certain nationalism in schooling may not rest solely in the exclusion of non-British culture, and 'English Studies' may be no more liberating if reformulated according to the requirements of multiculturalism. (Bhattacharyya 1991: 18)

If multiculturalism just sets up a slightly enlarged version of the nation, then marks it off as final, and settles down to enjoy its newly inclusive version of national identity, it too will have failed the test set by the performative's introduction of temporal disjunction. The marks of cultural difference which 'DissemiNation' considers, minority discursive performative acts, 'will not [...] celebrate the monumentality of historicist memory, the sociological totality of society, or the homogeneity of cultural experience'. (LC: 157) This observation goes for curricula in general, not only history curricula, for it is of course one characteristic of the US and English education systems, among others, that they have been driven towards 'the national curriculum'. On Bhabha's logic, it is not necessarily what gets taught that is the problem, more the very form of a standardized, falsely consensual, national curriculum. Educational theorist Michael W. Apple, citing Bhabha, puts this concisely in the US context: '[The national curriculum] may be modified by the conflicts that its content generates, but it is in its very establishment that its politics lies.' (Apple 1996: 35) The national narrative, in its forms of knowledge, is exemplary of larger educational questions. It does not matter who claims such knowledge, for it is the non-processual nature of that knowledge, claiming to know all it needs to know, to grasp the nation as it is and always will be, that is the problem.

SUMMARY

Bhabha's work is widely recognized for its emphasis on hybrid identities, diasporas, migrancy, and border-crossings. However figurative or literary this emphasis often is, it unquestionably implies a critical stance towards national institutions and nationalism. Many critics, in fact, assume that Bhabha is extremely hostile to nationalism, at least. However, Bhabha's perspective is more nuanced than that: although he is interested in the 'narrated' or 'imagined' qualities of nations, this does not necessarily imply that the narration or imagination in question is a bad thing. The identity of a nation is something narrated, but the process is two-fold: there is a pedagogical dimension that foregrounds total sociological facts, and there is a performative dimension reminding us that those total facts are always open, and in fact are being subtly altered every day. We are told what the nation is (and who is part of it), but at the same time the national subjects are inventing the nation at every moment, changing its ideas of itself as well as its institutions.

Although the pedagogical is apparently negative, it would not be correct to suggest that all emphasis is on the performative. It would be more accurate to argue that there is an oscillation between the two. As with almost all the structures described and produced in his work, Bhabha's thinking about the nation re-emphasizes temporality, the non-identical qualities of the nation, best explored by its minority groups. This has been the focus of much debate in the UK — for example, in the Parekh Report, which suggests that the pedagogical needs to incorporate a performative dimension. The everyday production of national newness has to be recognized and encouraged, and in this process teaching will play an important role.

7

CULTURAL RIGHTS

INTRODUCTION

The previous chapter focused on ways in which national narratives are disrupted. However, we cannot stop at the boundaries of individual nations, and this chapter draws out the lessons of such disruption for international contexts, particularly the language of human rights. As you have seen, Bhabha's work complicates our understanding of majority and minority identities, and this complication has clear implications for majority and minority *cultures*. His most recent work explores the connection between discourses of culture and discourses of human rights by focusing on cultural rights, which are guaranteed by international agreement. Bhabha argues that, while such international agreements are important, the very fact that they are (necessarily) agreements between nations means they neglect the rights of cultures that are *not* national. The experience of such cultures demands a transformation of human rights discourse.

Any discussion of cultural rights will have to face the complexity of the term culture itself, which is one of those words that come to us too easily, despite the elusiveness of their meanings. We use it in all manner of ways, many of which are mutually exclusive. It is, so Marxist cultural theorist Raymond Williams has written, 'one of the two or three most

complicated words in the English language'. (Williams 1983: 87)
Intuitively, any claim to cultural rights will most likely be rather complex in itself. Due to the complexities of the post-colonial, globalized
world, the frameworks put in place after 1945 to defend human rights
have come under increasing strain. For Bhabha, minority perspectives
can revitalize these frameworks. Essentially, he contends that the post-
colonial perspective should be privileged when it comes to discussing
human rights. That perspective can be understood in terms of the
parallax, meaning an apparent change in the position of an object when
the person looking at the object changes position. In this case the object
is culture, and the post-colonial parallax view has important implications for how we think about culture, cultures, multiculturalism, and
other related issues.

CULTURE AND HYBRIDITY

Contemporary culture is hybrid, just like colonial culture. The idea of
hybridity usefully characterizes the mechanisms of the colonial psychic
economy. In the same way as the structures of colonial identity can
also be found in contemporary contexts, the structure of hybridity is
also found in contemporary cultures. The important point to recognize is that cultures are always *retrospective* constructions, meaning that
they are consequences of historical process. Accordingly, when we
come to study hybridity, we need appropriate critical forms.
Interviewed for the journal *Art in America*, Bhabha suggests the following about his own writing:

> The post-colonial perspective resists attempts at holistic forms of social
> explanation. I question the traditional liberal attempt to negotiate a coming
> together of minorities on the basis of what they have in common and what is
> consensual. In my writing, I've been arguing against the multiculturalist
> notion that you can put together harmoniously any number of cultures in a
> pretty mosaic. You cannot just solder together different cultural traditions to
> produce some brave new cultural totality. The current phase of economic
> and social history makes you aware of cultural difference *not* at the celebra-
> tory level of diversity but always at the point of conflict or crisis. (ANI: 82)

This passage brings together various important assumptions. As you will recall, Bhabha refuses totalizing explanatory schemes, and here he associates such schemes directly with one version of multiculturalism, which attempts to weld disparate cultures into harmonious wholes. Really, however, the last sentence is recalling us to the fact that those disparate cultures are in no way pre-existing, but are an effect of historical change, specifically of colonialism and post-colonialism: that is what is implied by the 'point of conflict or crisis'. Cultural hybridity is not, then, something absolutely general. Hybridity may appear to go all the way down, in all cultures, but that would blur all difference into indifference, making all hybridity appear the same. Bhabha's theory of hybridity is associated with mimicry and sly civility (see Chapter 4), but is also importantly a denial that there were cultures already there that became hybrid. This point becomes clear in the following long quotation from the essay 'Signs Taken For Wonders':

> [C]olonial hybridity is not a *problem* of genealogy or identity between two *different* cultures which can then be resolved as an issue of cultural relativism. Hybridity is a problematic of colonial representation and individuation that reverses the effects of the colonialist disavowal, so that other 'denied' knowledges enter upon the dominant discourse and estrange the basis of its authority – its rules of recognition. Again, it must be stressed, it is not simply the *content* of disavowed knowledges – be they forms of cultural otherness or traditions of colonialist treachery – that return to be acknowledged as counter-authorities. For the resolution of conflicts between authorities, civil discourse always maintains an adjudicative procedure. What is irremediably estranging in the presence of the hybrid – in the revaluation of the symbol of national authority as the sign of colonial difference – is that the difference of cultures can no longer be identified or evaluated as objects of epistemological or moral contemplation: cultural differences are not simply *there* to be seen or appropriated. (LC: 114)

This passage stresses two things. First, we do not start with two or more cultures, more or less pure, and then trace their historical movements of hybridization. In the colonial situation, the production of cultures is an inevitable consequence of contested authority. For example, this essay investigates attempts to impose the so-called English Book (the Bible, but the language more generally as well). In Bhabha's reading, an apparently absolute cultural difference is actually a product of the strategies adopted by both sides in this story. In different ways, the two different cultures are 'not the *source* of conflict' but are instead 'the *effect* of discriminatory practices'. (LC: 114) We have to recognize that cultures are effects of stabilization produced by authority, but that recognition does not deny them reality.

The second point will be familiar by now. If we are to take this shift of emphasis into account, then we cannot take discussions of cultural difference at face value, and we cannot write as if there really were or are different cultures out there for us to study disinterestedly and discretely. As in the case of the stereotype, Bhabha believes that hybridity calls into question traditional analyses of colonialism, which tend to merely reverse the terms of colonial knowledge. These two points are linked again in an interview titled 'The Third Space', which makes direct connections between colonial discourse and the post-colonial 'third space':

> [F]or me the importance of hybridity is not to be able to trace two original moments from which the third emerges, rather hybridity to me is the 'third space' which enables other positions to emerge. This third space displaces the histories that constitute it, and sets up new structures of authority, new political initiatives, which are inadequately understood through received wisdom. (TS: 211)

Bhabha contends that hybridity is not a consequence of other, allegedly 'pure' positions thrust together. Hybridity is not the consequence of dialectical sublation, in other words a synthesis of thesis and antithesis, as discussed in Chapter 2. Further, what Bhabha so often implies about the logical structure of the dialectic has more practical relevance. Academic disciplines, for example, are effects of disciplinary stabilization, but this does not mean that they can be dismissed. (TT: 118) More generally, just as in Hegel, Marx, and many other thinkers, the logical structure of hybridity is not merely logical, but has pertinence to the understanding of social structures. This crossover between the logical and the socio-political is something that Bhabha has explored particularly in relation to human rights issues, as this chapter will explore. Before more in-depth discussion of rights, it is useful to consider the following quotation from 'The Postcolonial and the Postmodern'. If it seems familiar, that will be because an earlier version was discussed at the beginning of this book, when I suggested it introduced the central themes of Bhabha's work. If you compare the two passages, perhaps the most obvious thing you will notice is what is added here, in the final two sentences:

> Current debates in postmodernism question the cunning of modernity – its historical ironies, its disjunctive temporalities, its paradoxes of progress, its representational aporia. It would profoundly change the values, and judgements, of such interrogations, if they were open to the argument that metropolitan histories of civitas cannot be conceived without evoking the savage colonial antecedents of the ideals of civility. It also suggests, by implication, that the language of rights and obligations, so central to the modern myth of a people, must be questioned on the basis of the anomalous and discriminatory legal and cultural status assigned to migrant, diasporic, and refugee populations. Inevitably, they find themselves on the frontiers between cultures and nations, often on the other side of the law. (LC: 175)

In a complexly globalized world, the international language of rights seems to challenge the focus on the nation-state. This language also implicitly questions the metropolitan historicist narratives to which Bhabha refers here as elsewhere. However, this same language of rights develops out of liberal assumptions about internationalism, seen as precisely what the term suggests: the interplay of pre-existent nations, and, in terms of cultural rights, of national cultures. Bhabha's concern is that many of the people who would intuitively most require protection are not adequately covered by this language, precisely because they cannot be so easily and neatly located within any national culture. Accordingly, if the post-colonial perspective assists in the revision of metropolitan narratives, in a similar way the migrant perspective demands that we re-think the possession of rights. It suggests that a truly transnational culture of rights is still to be built.

LIBERALISM AND MINORITY RIGHTS

Alongside the increasing complexification of international human rights discourse and legal provision, over the last fifteen years there has been increased liberal philosophical development of frameworks concerning minority rights. In order to clarify how Bhabha's thought can contribute to the debate over minority rights, this section will briefly discuss one influential political philosopher, Will Kymlicka. Kymlicka's thought operates in a framework of nations, and his conception of minority rights works against certain notions of the nation as *neutral* space. Instead of assuming that a nation's institutions are ethno-culturally neutral, Kymlicka argues that it is important to acknowledge that there is a process of *nation-building* at work, producing what he calls *societal cultures*: 'a territorially-concentrated culture, centred on a shared language which is used in a wide range of societal institutions, in both private and public life (schools, media, law, economy, government, etc.)'. (Kymlicka 2001: 25) Demands for minority rights are reactions to this generally invisible or unremarked nation-building process, and so are less about special treatment than about equal opportunity. These demands are, he suggests, entirely consistent with classic liberal principles. Kymlicka summarizes his position as follows: 'All else being equal, national minorities should have the same tools of nation-building available to them as the majority nation, subject to the same liberal limitations.' (2001: 29)

This debate takes place in terms of the nation, and operates with at least minimal reference to practical policy. Given this emphasis, Kymlicka's examples are what he imagines to be 'standard' cases, and he specifies three main patterns of minority rights demands: ethnoreligious sects, immigrants, and national minorities. Many other cases, Kymlicka acknowledges, are considerably more complicated than these three main, standard examples. He refers to these complex cases as 'in-between' cases. However, he suggests, the standard cases will help us think about the complex in-between cases because 'the demands of in-between groups are often a complex hybrid of different (and sometimes contradictory) elements drawn from the more familiar models of ethnoreligious marginalization, immigrant integration, and separatist nationalism'. (2001: 31) In other words, we should look to the middle of the spectrum for our lessons in minority rights. These standard examples will contain all the constituent elements to be found in more complex cases. This use of examples would not seem quite so obvious to Bhabha. Certainly Bhabha's work as a whole reminds us to question where we look for our lessons, very often recommending the post-colonial perspective as the most insightful. Additionally, Bhabha will question the defaulting of discussion into nation-state terms. Both of these points about minority rights are present in Bhabha's work on colonial and post-colonial literary–cultural discourse. What he argues about rights extends his thought's implications explicitly into law. It is interesting that Kymlicka should use the term 'hybrid' to characterize the complex cases which might lead us astray. Bhabha's sense of hybridity would not only refer to the complexity of certain demands for rights, but also to the complexly hybrid histories from which those demands issue.

Hybridization is banal, it is everyday, and so many of the least extreme examples can quite easily focus debate on minority rights. And yet hybridization is not just everyday banality, especially not in terms of international law. Those extreme, in-between cases that Kymlicka opts to put to one side are perhaps not merely complex mixed-up versions of those cases he does consider. In certain ways, those cases, often suspended in-between nations, are not just exceptions but increasingly the norm, especially for a language of human rights that should operate transnationally rather than internationally. Minority rights can and must be thought of in terms of national frameworks, as Kymlicka explores, but they must also be thought of in terms that exceed nations, precisely because so many people are being written off as *excessive* to nations. The problem is best posed, it would seem, in terms of cultural rights, and this is where Bhabha makes his contribution. If cultures are, on Bhabha's view, the consequence of hybridizing processes, then this view necessitates a rethinking of the kinds of international agreement exemplified by the Universal Declaration of Human Rights.

Essentially, Bhabha sees such agreements as analogous to traditional historical approaches to colonialism, in that they concede far too much to the perspectives they are apparently designed to challenge. Article

27(1) of the Universal Declaration, specifically protecting cultural rights, says the following:

> Everyone has the right freely to participate in the cultural life of the community, to enjoy the arts and to share in scientific advancement and its benefits.

The status of this 'community' is apparently open, but easily tends towards the national community. Legal philosopher Costas Douzinas makes the following comment about the production of human rights discourse in the period after 1945: 'While the major powers fought tooth and nail over the definitions and priorities of human rights, they unanimously agreed that these rights could not be used to pierce the shield of national sovereignty.' (Douzinas 2001: 185) This problem has particular importance when it comes to cases in, for example, a war crimes tribunal. The International Criminal Court was set up by treaty in 1998, and yet the US (and six other countries) voted against the treaty, apparently because of fears that politically motivated accusations would be made against US troops. In other words, the priority of the nation remains in place, and is potentially impeding the processes of justice. This priority is a problem in a rather different way for Bhabha. For Bhabha, Article 27 of the Universal Declaration operates on the assumption that there are well-defined and bounded cultures out there in the world, and this assumption has various implications that Bhabha works against in recent articles, which I will draw together here.

In the essay 'On Minorities: Cultural Rights', Bhabha begins with two terms from philosopher Charles Taylor, who writes in terms of the 'whole society' being achieved through the exclusion of 'partial milieux' (it is worth recalling that in 'Signs Taken For Wonders', hybridity is described as a 'partializing process' and 'a metonymy of presence'. (LC: 115)) On this view a whole society is essentially a national society, achieved through the assimilation of minority identities, thought of as 'partial milieux'. In much the same way, Article 27, Bhabha suggests, places emphasis on the preservation of majoritarian identities at the expense of the minoritarian. Article 27, it seems, is unconcerned with the production of minoritarian identity, implying rather that such identity is an *excess* that is to be constantly assimilated. This assimilation is the kind of consequence of the dialectic that Bhabha wishes to resist. However, given the alleged focus of such international agreements, they seem rather too quick to take nation-state organizations as natural. This may just recall us to the fact that international agreements are precisely that: agreements between nations. None the less, the other sense of 'between nations' is what Bhabha is concerned about: people who are, for various reasons, between nations legally, culturally, or otherwise. These in-between people are not just marginal examples, unimportant to the central business of human rights discourses. In fact, 'partial milieux', although seemingly destined only for assimilation, are increasingly both intra- and internationally central. Accordingly, if cultures are to be protected, they cannot only be national cultures, as is becoming only more obvious because of social and political developments on both national and global scales.

Bhabha's ideas about the hybrid and the national transform cultural rights discussion. If we return to the narration of the nation, it is important to remember that its movements are simultaneously pedagogical and performative. Elsewhere I suggest that the performative is usually valued over and against the pedagogical, although Bhabha is sometimes clear that both are necessary, and this valuation is again the case in his thoughts on cultural rights, a precarious balance also necessary in the explicitly related question of individual and collective rights. Here Bhabha writes that 'The property of the human being is the collective or the transindividual construction of her or his individual autonomy; and the value of human agency arises from the fact that no one can be liberated by others, although no one can liberate herself or himself without others.' (OM: 6) Another way of making this point is to say that human rights discourses and institutions require both a kind of poetic individualism and a governing, administrative rationality. That which exceeds legal frameworks, and that which poetically figures the individual's irreducibility to mere example of a group, is simultaneously gathered in via a shuttling motion to the administrative and the pedagogical. What Bhabha argues about the minoritarian perspective gestures towards how hybridity might re-write concrete legislation, but at the same time Bhabha does not spell out the practical implications of his thought:

> The creation of new minorities reveals a liminal, interstitial public sphere that emerges *in-between* the state and the non-state, *in-between* individual rights and group needs; not in the simpler dialectic between global and local. Subjects of cultural rights occupy an analytic and ethical borderland of 'hybridization' in a partial and double identification across minority milieux. In fact, the prevailing school of legal opinion specifically describes minority cultural rights as assigned to 'hybrid' subjects who stand somewhere in-between individual needs and obligations, and collective claims and choices, in partial milieux. (OM: 4–5)

As in the narration of the nation, there are questions of both essence and practice, or pedagogy and performance. The minoritarian perspective entails a thinking of what Bhabha elsewhere thinks of as the social as processual or performative, linking these two terms that, as I have suggested, recur throughout his work. Bhabha's article actually distinguishes between *thinking* the problem and *describing* it. The first is a matter for poetry, the second for law. Again we are invited to see a difference between intervening in a situation and just describing the situation. The poetic translation of the partial, dependent identification of the minority is without question the former: the minoritarian is not a matter of essence (pedagogy) but of practice (performance). If this elevation of the poetic seems to be a little surprising in this context, the next section gives more detail of how Bhabha views the strange alignment of discrepant possibilities achievable through poetic licence, by giving a detailed reading of one of his recent talks.

WRITING RIGHTS

In the context of cultural rights, Bhabha's work requires us to retain both the performative and the pedagogical dimensions of culture. In his Oxford Amnesty Lecture, titled 'On Writing Rights', the pedagogical is on the side of law and the performative is on the side of literature. However, just as in the case of national narration, this is no simple polarity. Bhabha asks, 'Can the culture of rights and the writing of culture be made to converse with each other, to convey, in collaboration, the human spirit?' (WR: 164) It is well to point out that his criticisms of human rights discourse are in no way a dismissal of that discourse. The categories of rights and writing can and indeed must be brought together constructively.

Once again, Bhabha considers Taylor's thoughts on partial milieux. Remember that Taylor conceives of respect due to 'whole' societies, their wholeness partially dependent on longevity and holism. For Bhabha, Taylor's conception is but the latest example of how human rights discourse betrays 'an inability to conceive of the "cultural options of the minority" outside of the national, even nationalist, frame'. (WR: 166) The national is always implied in references to whole societies, in other words. There is, in fact, a 'prescriptive imperative to nationhood and national culture' (WR: 167), evidenced by early (failed) attempts by some nations to amend the Universal Declaration so that immigrants would not be considered minorities. Article 27 still, however, elevates a notion of stability for minority cultures that remains removed from the realities of many partial milieux. The Universal Declaration, of course, is what it says it is: universal, and so applicable to humans everywhere. But matters may not be so simple. Although emphasis on the most general level of being human, the 'merely human', would seem to forestall any recourse to discourses of nationalism, Bhabha maintains that behind this apparently most general vocabulary there is a familiar figure: 'it is my view that behind the "universal" language of the merely human there is a very specific idea of a "national" culture that becomes the inevitable basis of cultural judgement and cultural justice'. (WR: 170) Even if the figure of the nation is only implied, it is still thereby installed as some kind of normative category. There is an unspoken expectation that we will all belong to a nation, in some way. However, clearly we do not all belong to nations in the same way, and those of us who do are intuitively least likely to require the protection of the Universal Declaration. Further, there are other problems related to this implicit presence of the nation in a discourse of supposed absolute generality, and once again they are problems of *time*. The problem is one of what Bhabha calls, summarizing legal philosopher Joseph Raz, 'tension in the creation of community'. (WR: 171) Of course, as you will remember, tense negotiation – agonism – is for Bhabha both necessary and ongoing.

In Chapter 6, I explained that the migrant's perspective can be envisaged as simultaneously a problem and an opportunity. While we should not romanticize the migrant – and should always remember that there is no *one* kind of migrant – we should remain open to the perspectives opened by experiences of migrancy. Unsurprisingly, for Bhabha there is a lesson for human rights culture in the problems of minority cultures. All the way through this book I have argued that Bhabha's emphasis is always on processes, and this is again the case for cultural rights. Minority cultures have, he writes, 'a profound sense of the partial and the processual in the self-fashioning of political subjecthood and cultural identification'. (WR: 168) Our lessons in process are best learned from the post-colonial and the minoritarian perspectives.

To see how Bhabha explains this process, we must look again to dictionary definitions, this time of the 'mere' to which we refer when we say 'merely human'. The *Shorter Oxford English Dictionary* gives us our everyday sense of 'nothing less than', or 'nothing more than'. It also gives us the archaic or dialectal sense of 'boundary' or 'landmark', sometimes even a 'green balk or road, serving as a boundary'. Bhabha is interested in possible interplay between the modern and archaic meanings, although he does not mention the sense of a *road* serving as a boundary, a sense which helpfully reinforces what he wants to say. He argues that 'We continually shuttle between these two meanings in the making of culture – the human as an ethical or moral horizon beyond everyday life, and the human as constituted through the process of historical and social time.' (WR: 170) This structure is again that of the pedagogical and the performative, the former associated with universal humanity, the latter with humanity on the move, in the everyday. Universal categories are necessary constructions that we know will necessarily fail to cover every last instance or example of individual human agency. There needs to be a translation between the two levels of description. This translation or shuttling is precisely the movement that I suggested characterized Bhabha's understanding of the national narrative. You will remember that the pedagogical seemed to be all that was necessary for the sense of the nation-people, but that it was continually drawn into an economy of the performative, and the same is true here: 'In complex multicultural societies, the "culture of humanity" requires that we continually translate the "merely" human, the more metaphysical sense of meaning and identity, into "mere humanity" as the border between various social and historical forces that produce the "human" as a multicultural category'. (WR: 171) There is a need to hold onto both senses of being human, which will allow the open poetic becoming of culture to coexist with its necessary institutional defence. Minority group rights have to hold on to both individual and group levels.

GENDER AND GROUP RIGHTS

Of course there are various objections to the idea of special minority group rights, often concerning alleged neglect of the individual level. These are usually framed in narrowly national terms, as they must often be, but Bhabha's thought has relevance to that debate too. Most familiarly, many liberal thinkers question the defence of minority cultures when these cultures apparently conflict with majority attitudes. This conflict is usually explained by reference to gender issues – you might think about the French ban on 'overt religious symbols' in schools, which so often focuses on the hijab. Even if majorities in liberal states (in this debate usually assumed to be 'Western') continue gender discrimination in practice, there is still formal and legal provision for gender equality. Many liberals suggest there is a clash between this formal gender equality and special rights granted to cultural groups.

A good example of this position is the question asked by Susan Moller Okin (1997): 'Is multiculturalism bad for women?' Okin engages specifically with Kymlicka's work. Her suggestion is that feminism and multiculturalism are not necessarily easily reconciled. Why does she make this claim? Okin argues that, although minority groups would still be fulfilling the same criteria as the majority culture when it comes to the public sphere (politics), there are no guarantees of that fulfilment in the private sphere (the home). In other words, because gender inequality is often a feature of the private sphere, for example in terms of reproduction, it is possible that group rights will defend gendered cultures – minority cultures that can be much more heavily gendered than the majority liberal culture. Okin looks to examples like child marriage and polygamy, around which minority cultures come into direct conflict with majority liberal cultures. These cultural phenomena, continues Okin, may be defended by the (often male/ageing) leadership of a minority culture, but women (particularly young women) often see them in a different light. Okin suggests that, 'by failing to protect women and sometimes children of minority cultures from male and sometimes maternal violence, cultural defences violate their rights to the equal protection of the laws'. In other words, cultural rights are potentially in conflict with individual legal rights.

Kymlicka himself responds to Okin's argument. His position is that group rights are only permissible when they are claimed to defend a vulnerable minority culture against the majority culture. They are not permissible if they impose restrictions within the minority cultural group. (Kymlicka 1997) Bhabha's response to Okin is quite different. Elsewhere he discusses the importance of the domestic sphere in the rewriting of law, politics, and the public sphere. (CM: 584) Bhabha obviously, then, has sympathy for aspects of Okin's argument; however, he suggests that Okin's perspective is comparable to that of patriarchal minority group leaders, in that she imagines minority groups to be external to or isolated from 'the great storm of Western progress'. (LSC) Minority cultures are, Bhabha suggests, given essential identities which mean they are never quite part of present historical processes, but are projected as existing in different times and places. Instead of seeing minority cultures as being part of the same processes as majority cultures, there is an implied distance in Okin's position. She then casts all relations between liberal majorities and minority cultures in terms of conflict, missing the liberalisms already present within minority cultures. These minority liberalisms have, Bhabha insists, for a long time debated the *de facto* inequalities that continue in Western liberal cultures, whatever their legal provisions for equality. More importantly, these minority liberalisms are examples of cultures on the move, progressing in ways that are not simply measurable against the standards of Western liberalism. Of course there is nothing to stop the leaders in any given culture defining that culture as just as stable and fixed as nationalism claims nations to be. The question asks who gets to tell a culture's stories. Although it has been argued that his work neglects gender issues (for example, McClintock 1995: 64–5), here at least Bhabha engages with the question of who controls the definitions of any culture. Bhabha is making the case for recognizing the processes animating minority cultures, implying a right to free up the stories told about those cultures, and the standards by which they might be judged. In short, he is discussing minority cultures in terms of a *right to narrate*.

RIGHT TO NARRATE

Bhabha positions his understanding of cultural rights, then, in terms of cultures on the move – cultures as being narrated. Accordingly, he has repeatedly written of a right to narrate, which the following section will explore. Perhaps we casually associate narration with prose, specifically prose fiction, but Bhabha develops his notion of the right to narrate through repeated recourse to Adrienne Rich's poem 'Inscriptions' (1995). Bhabha quotes Rich's poem in various contexts, but always with an eye to its insertion of the second person into the first, that is, its introduction of the temporal dimension. He is not bending Rich's poem in any way, for it is a meditation on the individual and belonging, specifically around questions of 'Race class … all that'. Bhabha suggests that Rich's poem shows us 'that to belong to a movement, in the collective or political sense of the word, demands a renewed sense of self-recognition that disturbs the language of self and Other, of individual and group'. (WR: 172) In other words, to belong to a movement is also to be in movement, in process. Bhabha refers to 'a negotiated (un)settlement [...] between the subject as first person – I – confronted by its split double – You – that is future's part, the politicized "person to come" '. (WR: 174) Here we see yet another doubling, another self not quite at one with itself, and the structure is strangely enough just that of the discourse of man confronted by its doubles. Through Rich's poem Bhabha evokes the sense in which cultural rights are not a question of multicultural rights, but of *inter*cultural rights. Rich works to open 'the space of what I call a chiasmatic, diagonally crossed, lateral "side-by-side" solidarity where differences do not aspire to be represented in sovereign autonomy'. (WR: 175) Differences, like national identities, are not sociological facts, or absolute horizons of meaning – although they are relative horizons, of course. And Rich herself makes one of Bhabha's most repeated points again for him, for class is made one among many elements of difference, to be brought together, without guarantees, in a politics that is 'a process of making connections between partial cultural milieux'. (WR: 174)

So, thematically Rich's poem coincides with many of Bhabha's most insistent concerns. However, I have already raised the question of its formal qualities: bluntly, it is a poem, and although there are many narrative poems we would perhaps more usually associate narrative with prose narrative. Indeed, Bhabha perhaps concedes as much when he brings his Amnesty Lecture to a close through the example of Toni Morrison's *Paradise* (1999), through which he suggests that 'narrative invests language with the "right" to explore and endure, to survive and savour a complex revision in the community of meaning and being'. (WR: 179–80) *Paradise* tells the story of an all-black town called Ruby, a town founded by the descendants of free slaves. The town's isolated patriarchal culture is threatened by its ironic double, a community of women living in a nearby abandoned convent. The novel turns on questions of authenticity and tradition, focused around the Oven, the heart of the community where its baptisms take place, which was moved from the town's original location called Haven. The Oven has assumed mythical value, particularly the ambiguity of its near-illegible engravings. Reading Morrison's novel, particularly the focus on the shifting value of the Oven between Haven and Ruby, one gets a strong sense of what Bhabha is arguing here. The debate over the Oven's motto, whether or not it needs 'clarification', is hardly decisively settled. This debate also concerns the 'meaning' or identity of Ruby as community, and the following passage nears Bhabha's own position: 'Specifying it, particularizing it, nailing its meaning down, was futile.' (Morrison 1999: 93) That Bhabha finds such suggestive themes in Morrison's novel helps explain the blurring between narrative and literature in these closing sections of his lecture, but it is clear that he is making a strong case for literature's qualities as a supplement to law. More specifically, he is suggesting that literature is what gives the language of law access to the right to narrate, which is essentially a right of intervention in the telling of histories and, therefore, history happening *in the pages of* ... a novel, a poem, a newspaper story, even literary theory. The programmatic definition of that right is given as follows, and immediately broadens the scope of that narration, reminding us why it is appropriate that a poem as much as anything else should frame these theoretical reflections:

> By the 'right to narrate', I mean to suggest all those forms of creative behaviour that allow us to represent the lives we lead, question the conventions and customs that we inherit, dispute and propagate the ideas and ideals that come to us most naturally, and dare to entertain the most audacious hopes and fears for the future. The right to narrate might inhabit a hesitant brush stroke, be glimpsed in a gesture that fixes a dance movement, become visible in a camera angle that stops your heart. Suddenly in painting, dance, or cinema you rediscover your senses, and in that process you understand something profound about yourself, your historical moment, and what gives value to a life lived in a particular town, at a particular time, in particular social and political conditions. (WR: 180)

Narration is clearly being used in a broad sense, broad enough to take in not only novels and poetry, but also painting, dance, and photography. We know all these things are modes of narration, but it is worth remembering that Bhabha is not confining himself to words on the page. The above passage touches on many of the themes outlined in this book – defamiliarization, process, and the specificity of time and place. Through the course of this book it will have become obvious that Bhabha's work is interdisciplinary, in a basic sense. It touches on many different issues, through many different media. I have discussed poems, fiction, cinema, and photography, and not come near exhausting the range of Bhabha's reference. This question of range sends us right back to where we started, in Chapter 2, when I suggested that the meaning Bhabha finds in John Stuart Mill is already present and waiting to be found. Mill is not perhaps the best example because he would seem to be an antagonistic example – Bhabha's reading clearly transforms Mill's meaning. However, the other examples to which I have made reference suggest that the idea of twisting is not really relevant to Bhabha's method. The introduction of, or the telling reminder of, the temporal, or the processual, is really what the right to narrate is all about. When Bhabha refers to the right to narrate we are plunged into the language of rights, into covenants incomplete and declarations not adhered to; however, we are also recalled to the necessity of reinserting agonistic and disjunctively temporal elements into the discourse of rights, just as those elements need reinsertion into the analysis of colonial authority, or the discourse of the nation. Narrative is, Bhabha insists, 'a moving sign of civic life'. (WR: 181) If it is stifled, by those either against narration (who do not want the truth to be told) or those apparently in favour of its reassertion (who want only the unified truth, contradictions and negotiations excised), then the result is the monolith, the holistic total sociological explanation, or the authoritarian political culture: 'When you fail to protect the right to narrate, you are in danger of filling the silence with sirens, megaphones, hectoring voices carried by loudspeakers from podiums of great height over people who shrink into indistinguishable masses ...' (WR: 181)

'DE-REALIZING DEMOCRACY'

The situation he is describing may be unfolding again in the early twenty-first century. Indeed, Bhabha's more recent essays put his thought to the test of the post-9/11 world. Writing before 9/11, literary critic Marjorie Perloff suggests that, although there are many problems with his work, 'In its general outlines, Bhabha's hybridity paradigm has enormous appeal' (Perloff 1998); however, more recently she argues that the post-9/11 world proves the poverty of post-colonial theory, and specifically of Bhabha's work (Eakin 2001). She understands Bhabha as simply insisting on the hybridity of all cultures, and the ways in which cultures are not polarized, facing off against each other. If that is the case, Perloff suggests, the apparently polarizing world-views now evident undermine the post-colonial argument. Such a perspective has been common, if not uncontested. It operates in terms of the controversial thesis, elaborated by Samuel Huntington from the work of Bernard Lewis, that this century will witness a clash of civilizations (1997). This book has already suggested that, for Bhabha, hybridity is banality, it is the everyday. Further, contrary to received wisdom his work is interested in the moments of clash, of polarization, and of stasis. It is unsurprising that he has offered thoughtful comments on this supposed clash of civilizations. I will now explain his essay 'Democracy De-Realized' as an example of how he questions a cultural racism that divides the world into discrete cultural *spaces*: again, Bhabha wants to reinsert a *temporal* dimension into ongoing debates.

The essay begins by outlining our apparent situation, although this word 'our' implies the pre-existent divisions between self and other that the essay challenges, and so has to be qualified. In the contemporary moment, we are often offered 'the stark choice of civilizational clash – between Faith and Unfaith, or Terror and Democracy'. (DD: 31) The responses to processual truth outlined in the previous section are two aspects of the same attitude, and therefore remind us that what Bhabha calls 'the embattled and embalmed narrative of civilizational clash' (DD: 27) is really a narrative without movement, and without opposition. What Bhabha argues about cultural rights gets to the heart of the post-9/11 world picture, or more precisely to the heart of many tendentious theories of that world picture, particularly that revitalized thesis of civilizational clash. Importantly, the implications of his work are far more interesting and far-reaching than a slightly facile acknowledgement of cultural hybridity. The context of 9/11 gives Bhabha an opening to consider how the clash of civilizations thesis undermines the careful attention and self-

situation that his work recommends. Huntington's thesis is comparable to Marxist analysis of contradiction as the 'motor of history': this
analysis installs an inevitable and dangerous *telos* (historical or philosophical destiny) to be pursued at all costs, meaning that the real
interests of the working class have been (for example, in the Soviet
Union) overridden in favour of theoretical interests laid out by
Marxism. Huntington's thesis (although by now it is not his only)
tries to tidy up the complexity of global cultures by mapping political actions onto invented and stable cultures: real cultures are locked
into a theory, even if that theory does not predict the consequences
of the clash of civilizations.

Against this invention, in a familiar gesture which reminds us to be
careful in our choice of examples, Bhabha insists that the best place
to learn our lessons regarding democracy is not where democracy is
most vociferously proclaimed, but rather where it has been most
ambiguous or even damaging in its effects: 'when faced with the crises
of progress or the perils of democracy, our lessons of equality and justice are best learned from those marginalized, peripheralized peoples
who have harvested the bitter fruits of liberalism in its project of colonization and slavery, rather than those imperial nations and sovereign
states that claim to be the seed-beds of Democracy'. (DD: 28) Things
are never quite as new as they seem, and things are never simply new:
'Unless we recognize what is old and weary about the world – those
"long histories" of slavery, colonization, diaspora – we are in no position
to represent what is emergent or "new" within our contemporary
global moment.' (DD: 30) The post-colonial perspective on democracy,
the parallax view from which democracy will appear so different, is a
matter of what Bhabha calls de-realization. He argues that it is imperative to de-realize democracy. The realization of democracy would be a
familiar enough goal: either democracy needs to be realized in as many
countries as possible, or we need to work hard to realize democracy
right here and right now, as previous efforts have been flawed. The term
de-realization is not, however, a mere play on this expected usage.
Bhabha uses the term 'de-realization' in two related ways. First, after
German dramatist Bertolt Brecht (1898–1956), it refers to 'a critical
"distance" or alienation disclosed in the very naming of the formation of

the democratic experience and its expressions of equality'. (DD: 29) In other words, at the moment when democracy is declared, it betrays evidence of excluded others. Second, in the manner of Surrealism, it means 'placing an object, idea, image or gesture in a context not of its making, in order to defamiliarize it, to frustrate its naturalistic and normative "reference" and see what potential that idea or insight has for "translation"'. (DD: 29) So, we also de-realize to disclose what democracy might be, instead of simply assuming we know what it should be. If we assume that we already know what democracy is, and what it can be in future, then we will be unready for what is coming from the future, the genuine changes that will come.

In the same way, Bhabha thinks that cosmopolitanism is always *to come* in a strong sense. Cosmopolitanism is not something that exists in the present, nor is it something that could exist fully in any present. It is not an object about which we have theories. Instead it is a *project*, like democracy: 'specifying cosmopolitanism positively and definitely is an uncosmopolitan thing to do'. (CM: 577) If we think we know what cosmopolitanism is, looking at it in terms of traditional Eurocentric intellectual history, for example beginning with its elaboration by German philosopher Immanuel Kant, then we limit ourselves to a specific kind of cosmopolitanism. This version of cosmopolitanism denies the constituent mediation in every culture, assuming it can partake of different and discrete, 'pure' cultures. It is very much a Eurocentric cosmopolitanism, and is inadequate for a world in which 'centers are everywhere and circumferences nowhere'. (CM: 588) Adequate to that world is what Bhabha calls a vernacular cosmopolitanism, or cosmopolitanism hybridized. This would begin by finding its cosmopolitan lessons in many cultural contexts, 'outside the box of European intellectual history'. (586) Cosmopolitanism would consequently be de-realized itself. This de-realization would be the beginning of a project to develop models of global citizenship. What we think we know about citizenship needs to be relativized, if we are not to produce further total theories that exclude vast numbers of people. We need to see that, when democracy is translated into 'other' contexts, it may be significantly transformed.

GLOBAL CITIZENSHIP

Throughout Bhabha's work, he argues that minority perspectives offer valuable lessons. Some examples just are the best examples of a given phenomenon, and when it comes to the strange case of the global subject, the post-colonial provides examples of the ongoing experience of transition. 'The territoriality of the global "citizen" is, concurrently, postnational, denational or transnational.' (DD: 30) This global citizen is difficult to describe. Bhabha's description of the phenomenon is maybe less important for the words it chooses than the relationship it sets up with the 'normal' case of nationality: its form is as least as important as its content. Bhabha discusses this citizenship in terms drawn from contemporary legal theory. Legal theorists have discussed what they call an 'effective nationality', a nationality that is *adjacent* to 'formal nationality'. This nationality would in principle have status in the context of international rights legislation. Although it would seem to be in a relationship of dependency or even subservience with formal nationality, its adjacency is less a poor substitute and more a necessary supplement. The global citizen is necessarily disjointed, not quite at one with itself. Effective nationality is, in other words, contiguous, and its relationship with formal nationality is one of metonymy.

This question of metonymy can be situated in the context of Bhabha's reading practice, and the mechanisms of the stereotype, as described in Chapters 2 and 3. Here, however, Bhabha is making connections with certain important influences on post-colonial criticism. He develops the work of Italian Marxist philosopher Antonio Gramsci (1891–1937), who is associated with the idea of *hegemony*. This is a concept that emphasizes the ways power is a matter not only of domination but also of consent. This consent is created through many different cultural means – mass media, for example. However, people do not just passively consume media images – they argue with them. In other words, in trying to create consent, hegemony encounters inevitable dissent. Accordingly, cultural meaning is negotiated, and is not something that can be simply imposed by ruling classes. But who conducts the negotiations? To answer this question, Bhabha evokes a 'philosophy of the part', a philosophy given institutional expression in the idea of 'the cultural front': 'A cultural front does not have a homogeneous and totalizing view of the world.' (DD: 31) The cultural front transforms the meaning of hegemony, because it undermines the idea of pre-given political identities. The relationships of hegemony may be complex negotiations, but they are still complex negotiations between fairly stable classes. Traditionally, you would know with some certainty which class you belonged to, and class has been how Marxism usually understands social relations. However, this certainty has disappeared, and politics is now a question of multiple competing identities, so that it is difficult to say which individual or collective identity is most important (are you working-class first, or a woman, or an environmental activist, etc.?). There is a need to *imagine* collective subjects, and not simply reduce these subjects to effects of rational contracts between fully conscious individuals: in other words, a cultural front is an alliance that is narrated, just like a nation.

Bhabha is specifically interested in how the hegemonic imagination is translated when coupled with Gramsci's idea of the *subaltern*. Indeed, it is through this latter category that Gramsci's influence is usually felt in post-colonial criticism, for example in the work of the Subaltern Studies group (see Guha 1998), Indian historians who challenged elite colonial historiography. Subalternity is also important in the work of Gayatri Chakravorty Spivak (1987; 1990; 1993; 1999), whose claim that the subaltern cannot speak has elicited continuing controversy. Bhabha emphasizes the ways in which subalternity is connected to the philosophy of the part: 'Subalternity represents a form of contestation or challenge to the status quo that does not homogenize or demonize the state in formulating an opposition to it.' (DD: 32) Rather than resorting to simplistic polarities, the cultural front places itself in a relationship of negotiation with the status quo: in other words, it does not simply reject the status quo. Instead, there is a demand for the recognition of process and partiality. The partializing presence, the metonymy that Bhabha apparently privileges over metaphor, is here refigured as subaltern contiguity, in other words a kind of translation between political contexts that is always provisional and ongoing. This provides a sound justification for grouping so many different experiences together as post-colonial: it is not to say that they are all 'the same', but to recognize that translations between contexts can be useful when transforming the status quo. But all these examples should perhaps, therefore, be marked as post-colonialisms *plural* rather than post-colonial *singular*.

Grouping these examples together constructs a form of counter-hegemony, i.e. a formation that attempts to substitute its understanding of the world for the status quo. Such a post-colonial cultural formation must be constructed with care, but its potential justifies that effort. This is because the post-colonial perspective has so many insights into the experiences that characterize the present. So, Bhabha suggests that the time of the contemporary, the feeling of time in the contemporary moment, is best imagined through the examples afforded by partial milieux, subjects and collectives who experienced those tired old histories of slavery and colonialism. He argues that 'The uneven and unequal playing field of the global terrain – "partial" and "incipient", neither past nor present but "incubational" – is nonetheless encountered and experienced as living in, and through, a shared historical time of "transition".' (DD: 31) It is this feeling of partiality and transition that should, for Bhabha, be built into the idea of global citizenship: the subaltern negotiates from a position of partiality, without the guarantees of age-old and rooted identity. Only through emphasizing the interconnectedness and incompleteness of our identities can we construct a model of citizenship that will not revert to default assumptions, e.g. concerning the permanence and pre-eminence of national identity.

In his essays about cultural rights, then, Bhabha takes many varied and unexpected paths, reading texts that seem superficially out of place. It seems that the form or the logic of these texts is what makes them attractive to him. Indeed, this book may have occasionally implied that Bhabha is curiously uninterested in the content of the texts he reads. That, at least, is how it sometimes appears, particularly to his critics. At any rate, in terms of rights his interest lies less in what is said than in the possibility of saying anything at all. This, he suggests, is a distinction between individual and collective rights: 'Freedom of expression is an individual right; the right to narrate, if you will permit me poetic license, is an enunciative right rather than an expressive right – the dialogic, communal or group right to address and be addressed, to signify and be interpreted, to speak and be heard, to make a sign and to know that it will receive respectful attention.' (DD: 34) In the end, then, the cultural right to narrate is a right to be read in a strong sense. The right to narrate is not being recognized in any interpretation that merely follows the standard, customary and conditioned rules, fitting whatever object is under consideration into the expected box, and thereby consigning it to eternal object-hood, without the possibility of its own subjectivity being accommodated.

SUMMARY

Cultures have not existed from time immemorial, as is sometimes implied. Nor do cultures exist in the present; they could not exist in any future present either. Cultures cannot be fully present: they are not a matter of being, but of becoming. Cultures are crafted, sculpted, or narrated objects: like traditions, cultures are invented. We might view this invention as a bad thing, to be deplored for its falsification of reality. Alternatively, we might want to grasp the positive potential in this invention of tradition, but only if we acknowledge that this invention will be ongoing. This is where Bhabha's idea of hybridity is important: it suggests that cultures come *after* the hybridizing process, rather than existing before. In colonial relationships, this is just as true of the colonizer as of the colonized. In the present, this should remind us that cultures are part of an *ongoing* process, which for Bhabha suggests that majority liberal cultures in the West must view themselves through the post-colonial perspective.

As this chapter went on to suggest, Bhabha's theoretization of hybridity has important consequences for discourses of rights. Minority cultures have tended to be ignored or, alternatively, asked to assimilate. Such has been the case even in the context of the grand narratives of human rights of the last fifty years, which have implicitly elevated national cultures as exemplary of ideal, 'whole' societies. However, such human rights culture might learn valuable lessons from the minority cultural emphasis on the processual, on the sense of politics as a matter of ongoing negotiation. Further, and finally, it has not been minority political culture alone that has explored and expanded our sense of trans-cultural possibilities: the right to narrate can in principle be found anywhere, as this book's discussions of cinema, photography, and literature suggest. We should not be too quick to dismiss any artefacts, nor too sure of our standard, commonsense readings of the world.

8

AFTER BHABHA

INTRODUCTION

In 1999 *Newsweek* magazine listed Bhabha as one of '100 Americans for the Next Century'. Bhabha has become something more than the everyday cultural critic, contributing to worldwide debates in contexts like the World Economic Forum. With his increased prominence have come increasingly animated debates over whether or not Bhabha actually deserves such distinction. In fact, the title of this chapter can be read in several ways. There are those who have written about Bhabha, some who have written in the manner of Bhabha, and those who have gone after him with theoretical scores to settle. Few critics of his prominence have been subject to so much adverse commentary, and accordingly much of this chapter will consider writers who have gone after Bhabha in the last sense. You will see that even the most critical commentators accept Bhabha's importance. Many, however, feel that the lessons of his work need serious qualification before they are turned once again to the colonial and neocolonial contexts. Indeed, for some critics, we are after Bhabha in the sense that we can do without his work and indeed theory generally — or at least we *ought* to be after Bhabha in this sense. To explore these different readings of Bhabha's influence, this chapter discusses representative or canonical examples of critical responses, rather than give endless lists of texts to which you might refer. However, almost every text in post-colonial studies references Bhabha's work at some point.

REVISING HISTORY: YOUNG

Robert J. C. Young is in many ways the most attentive writer to have followed Bhabha. His basic position is that we really should not expect Bhabha to write like someone else. As he has recently written: '[I]f Bhabha changed his interpretive methods in response to the objections of his critics, he would no longer be Bhabha, the brilliant insights would be lost, and he would become a conventional cultural or historical critic.' (2001: 347) And, more than likely, I would not be writing this book. Young's book *White Mythologies: Writing History and the West* (1990) contains one chapter devoted to Bhabha's work, but the entire book might be seen as an application of Bhabha's admonitions to stop thinking in historicist terms and start thinking historically. In this, it is also an application of certain lessons from Jacques Derrida's work (from which the title of Young's book is adapted), and so in another way it works alongside Bhabha, who also draws so much from Derrida. Thinking carefully through the implications of various Marxist versions of history, Young draws out the different ways in which they tend towards a certain colour-blindness. Working through Jean-Paul Sartre, Louis Althusser, and on to Fredric Jameson, Young questions the ways Marxism has constructed different versions of universal history, to the exclusion of colonized peoples. The later chapters of the book consider Bhabha's work alongside that of Edward Said and Gayatri Chakravorty Spivak, all of whom work to rewrite nominally universal history. Young's later book *Colonial Desire* (1995) takes its title from Bhabha's work, and considers all the ways in which the colonial archives are themselves littered with evidence of an obsession with categories of hybridity and syncretism; although the book warns against uncritically celebrating hybridity in our contemporary moment, its references to Bhabha are complimentary, demonstrating that Young has not misread Bhabha's own cautious formulations about such categories. Indeed, in the latter book Young famously refers to

Bhabha as one of the 'Holy Trinity' of post-colonial theory, alongside Edward Said and Gayatri Chakravorty Spivak.

Despite this characterization, Young's commentaries on Bhabha have always asked exactly the questions that much more vociferous critics have asked with increasing frequency in recent years. For example, *White Mythologies* wonders about the question of agency, particularly Bhabha's assertions about how we now might locate anti-colonial agency: 'documentary evidence of resistance by colonized peoples is not hard to come by, and is only belittled by the implication that you have to read between the lines to find it'. (1990: 149) Young accepts that Bhabha's work does not pretend that there was no resistance, or no resistance until the post-colonial critic came along and identified it; however, this leads Young to make the pertinent point that 'the more that Bhabha claims resistance, the less need there is for his psychoanalytic schema of fantasy and desire, narcissism and paranoia, in any analysis of the structures of colonialism'. (1990: 151) Many of the more forceful criticisms made of Bhabha's work can be found in Young, but because *White Mythologies* also asks such searching questions of Marxism, it has been easy to assume that Young accepts everything Bhabha writes without serious qualification.

Having said that, Young still believes that Bhabha's work is important. Young's most recent statement on the post-colonial is *Postcolonialism: An historical introduction* (2001), which he himself suggests is a reformulation of *White Mythologies*. The later book gives far more space to the classics or 'originals' of anti-colonial thinking, tracing all the ways in which Marxism was itself made hybrid from its beginnings. Bhabha is given respectful attention, but is now placed in a far more comprehensive set of historical and theoretical contexts. In particular, Young compares Bhabha's work with that of political psychologist Ashis Nandy, suggesting that there are parallels, influences and convergences of which we should be aware when we consider post-colonialism. Nandy's work, with its combination of Gandhi, psychoanalysis, and the critique of modernity, constructs a kind of counter-modernity, or what Young calls 'modernity hybridized'. (2001: 346) This characterization of course implies a thematic comparison with Bhabha's work. In fact, the comparison suggests not only thematic but also formal connections, as Young suggests when he writes that 'Both critics in their writing characteristically violate the historical integrity of the theoretical tradition from which they draw, and thereby deinstitutionalize its scope.' (2001: 347) The anachronistic reading method, which can look so disconnected from historical contexts, is on this view designed to jar the reader out of settled, institutionalized ways of thinking. As in Bhabha, Nandy's work implies that Marxism has been one of the most settled forms of institutionalized thinking, despite appearances. Marxism has remained static in fact, even if its theory is one of process, and both Nandy and Bhabha want to get things moving again.

POSTCOLONIALISM AS IDEOLOGY: AHMAD

Young's *White Mythologies* views Marxism as an extremely problematic discourse for post-colonialism, and in this it follows many of Bhabha's comments on Marxism. Notwithstanding Young's later nuanced history of post-colonialism, which places Marxism at the centre of the anti-colonial story, many Marxist critics have keenly felt the need to answer criticisms coming from post-colonial theory. Marxist literary critic Aijaz Ahmad is well known for his extremely critical views on post-colonial criticism, many of which are collected in *In Theory* (1992). Although he does not discuss Bhabha in that book, elsewhere he has made various dismissive remarks, particularly in the article 'The politics of literary post-coloniality'. In that article Ahmad refers to 'Bhabha's own assertion that explanations for human action must be non-rational'. (1995: 15) Ahmad understands Bhabha's vision of post-colonialism as almost hedonistic, and certainly irresponsible; he insists that the perspective that Bhabha calls post-colonial is rather more limited than Bhabha will allow. As with other critics of post-colonialism, Ahmad insists that the post-colonial critic is silently and unquestioningly assumed to be equivalent to a particular identity: 'In Bhabha's writing, the post-colonial who has access to such monumental and global pleasures is remarkably free of gender, class, identifiable political location. In other words, this figure of the post-colonial intellectual has a taken-for-grantedness of a male, bourgeois onlooker, not only

the lord of all he surveys but also enraptured by his own lordliness.'
(1995: 13) Ahmad's conclusion about Bhabha is the following:

> History does not consist of perpetual migration, so that the universality of
> 'displacement' that Bhabha claims both as the general human condition and
> the desirable philosophical position is tenable neither as description of the
> world nor as generalised political possibility. He may wish to erase the dis-
> tinction between commerce and revolution, between 'the mercantile and the
> Marxist', and he is welcome to his preferences; but that hardly amounts to a
> 'theory' of something called post-coloniality. Most individuals are really not
> free to fashion themselves anew with each passing day, nor do communities
> arise out of and fade into the thin air of the infinitely contingent. (1995: 16)

According to Ahmad, then, Bhabha's complication of oppositions,
say between merchants and Marxists, does not lead to a useful theory
of post-colonialism. If that hybridizing process is what characterizes
post-colonialism, indeed, then post-colonialism itself does not really
exist because in reality oppositions and restraints continue to govern
people's lives. This book has discussed several moments in Bhabha to
which this passage alludes, and has suggested that these moments are
not as simple as they appear. It would not be difficult to demonstrate
that Bhabha does *not* think perpetual migration is universal, that com-
merce and revolution are the same, or that communities are all absolutely vaporous. It would not be difficult to show, in other words, that
Ahmad's understanding of Bhabha is simplistic and reductive.

Indeed, although this book has emphasized the open-endedness of
cultural processes, this should not divert all attention away from
moments when cultures have quite legitimately and understandably
organized themselves around stable cultural forms. Bhabha is well
aware that cultural formations are not constantly on the move, and
that they come to a halt for many different reasons. As he says, some
people hold on to their cultural forms in an attempt at survival, and so
are 'caught in that margin of nonmovement within an economy of
movement'. (Clifford 1997: 43) Ahmad's sense that Bhabha simply
does not acknowledge this fact is not persuasive; his descriptions of
Bhabha's work seize on phrases, remove them from their contexts, so

making them unintelligible. It is a reading method that looks rather similar to Bhabha's own – the difference is Bhabha's loving attention to the texts he reads. Despite its problems, other critics have more persuasively presented some of the most searching aspects of Ahmad's position, as the following sections will show.

THE PROBLEM OF DISCOURSE: BENITA PARRY

The work of Benita Parry has reminded us that anti-colonial and nationalist writings were central in the struggles against colonial rule for a long time before post-colonialism ever appeared in Western universities. Her work has been a particularly good example of attacks on post-colonial theory that emphasize what it omits from its accounts of anti-colonialism, and Bhabha has been perhaps her main target. None the less, discussing Aijaz Ahmad's criticisms of post-colonialism (Salman Rushdie in particular), Parry makes the following comment which seems pertinent to Bhabha's work: 'a critical consciousness or a literary imagination alert to the crossing of borders and boundaries is not by definition indifferent to the diverse situations of those communities, without prestige or privilege, which not only experience but effect sea-changes in existing cultural formations'. (1987: 132) However, *indifference* is exactly what she diagnoses in Bhabha's work: the danger is, Parry suggests, that the attention to difference, if not tempered by acknowledgement of really existing structures and systems, will blur into indifference to the specific qualities of struggle in disparate times and places.

Parry develops her position in two important articles I will outline here; first, 'Problems in Current Theories of Colonial Discourse', which is a general consideration of colonial discourse analysis. Large parts of this essay compare the work of Spivak and Bhabha, particularly on the question of the 'subaltern voice', and it should be said that Parry's preference is for Bhabha's work: 'For Bhabha, the subaltern has spoken, and his readings of the colonialist text recover a native voice.' (1987: 40) However, the differences between Spivak and Bhabha are outweighed by their similarities. Perhaps Parry's main point can be explained by looking at how she reads Fanon. Her argument is that, although Fanon's colonized is the divided subject that Bhabha describes, and this division is anti-humanist, it is none the less also the case that this division is not a desirable quality: 'Fanon's writings intercede to promote the construction of a politically-conscious, unified revolutionary Self, standing in unmitigated antagonism to the oppressor, occupying a combative subject position from which the wretched of the earth are enabled to mobilize an armed struggle against colonial power.' (1987: 30) With this reading in mind, it is not surprising that Parry objects to Bhabha's apparent reading of Fanon as a premature post-structuralist: Parry understandably takes Bhabha's title ('Remembering Fanon', in the reissued *Black Skin, White Masks*) as offering something like a memory of what Fanon's work was really like, as opposed to a translation of Fanon. Parry objects to Bhabha's reading because it 'obscures Fanon's paradigm of the colonial condition as one of implacable enmity between native and invader, making armed opposition both a cathartic and a pragmatic necessity', (1987: 32) As you have seen in this book, Parry is quite right, although perhaps 'obscures' is not the right word, given that Bhabha explicitly replaces the one paradigm with his own (which is, none the less, Fanon's also) of non-binary opposition. Parry's reading, then, is not exactly a misreading, more a contestation of the consequences that follow Bhabha's critical movements; she feels that

> [... p]ositions against the nostalgia for lost origins as a basis for counter-hegemonic ideological production (Spivak), or the self-righteous rhetoric of resistance (Bhabha), have been extended to a down-grading of the anti-imperialist texts written by national liberation movements; while the notion of epistemic violence and the occluding of reverse discourses have obliterated the role of the native as historical subject and combatant, possessor of another knowledge and producer of alternative traditions. (1987: 34)

Parry's position, and it is one that Bhabha's writings often confirm, is that Bhabha seems to want to *replace* the actually existing texts and general practices of anti-colonialism. For Parry, such replacement has been what in practice has taken place in colonial discourse analysis. It is not that she absolutely dismisses Bhabha's work: instead, she wants to emphasize the limits of its productivity, what it can do for us. Those limits derive from an 'exorbitation of discourse and a related incuriosity about the enabling socio-economic and political institutions and other forms of social praxis'. (1987: 43) So, there are things external to discourse to which we have access, and to which colonial discourse analysis itself should pay attention, given that it assumes discourse itself as a set of practices. Parry's argument in this essay suggests that, with due attention to non-discursive practices, Bhabha's work could become more rounded, accommodating the long-standing insights of anti-colonial writers and activists. That is the broad outline of one objection to Bhabha's work; and now I will turn to criticisms of his specific reading of Fanon, to which Chapter 2 refers.

READING: NEIL LAZARUS

One critic whose position is extremely close to Parry's is Neil Lazarus. His book *Nationalism and Cultural Practice in the Postcolonial World* is in part a thoroughgoing critique of misrepresentations of nationalism in post-colonial theory. Lazarus's treatment of Bhabha focuses on that same, contentious reading of Fanon, which, for Lazarus, 'inverts the historical trajectory of Fanon's thought'. (Lazarus: 1999: 80) This inversion 'distort[s] the testimony of Fanon's own evolution as a theorist'. (1999: 79) Bhabha, Lazarus plausibly suggests, 'wishes to construct a portrait of Fanon as a poststructuralist *avant la lettre*'. (1999: 81) I have already shown that such a presentation, if it is indeed Bhabha's aim, is not quite so wildly implausible as has been suggested; however, Lazarus insists that contradictory textual evidence simply rules out this presentation, and that Bhabha is forced accordingly to misrepresent Fanon's thought, or to gently reprove Fanon for 'lapses'. Concerning the passages in which Bhabha teases out apparently impossible logics from Fanon's writing, Lazarus writes the following:

> The procedural logic of these passages is curious. Their thrust is to represent Fanon's ideas as according fundamentally with Bhabha's own epistemological and methodological program. To the extent that Fanon's explicit

formulations seem to render such a construction implausible, however, they need to be reproved for preventing Fanon from saying what he would have said, had he been able – that is, had he had the right words, or the time to reflect, or the courage to follow through his best insights. (1999: 81)

Lazarus is hardly making secret his contempt for this reading process, which for him is fundamentally a misreading. However, if this reading process was to be applied to, say, J. S. Mill, things might be different – 'what he would have said, had he been able', or more pertinently, 'what he said in spite of himself', seem to be most fitting characterizations of the outcomes of Bhabha's reading process. If we are on Fanon's side, as we ought to be, then, for Lazarus, 'the tendentiousness of Bhabha's appropriation of Fanon' (1999: 82) is little less than an insult to anti-colonial writers and activists. The distortion that Lazarus finds in Bhabha is not only of Fanon's own thinking, but is more general: it is a distortion of history. Lazarus does not emphasize what, I imagine, must be for him the most ironic element in Bhabha's reading: for someone who makes textuality all, Bhabha would seem to be rather cavalier with the textual evidence. However, that point would lead to various fraught questions regarding what texts do and their performative dimension, and Lazarus does not engage with that element of Bhabha's thinking. In fact, it might be argued that there is no obvious reason why the performative discursive acts of the past should be less significant than those of the present. Fanon is not only part of history, but has effects right here and now if we are prepared to really read him.

THE PROBLEM OF DIFFERENCE: BENITA PARRY

Parry's review essay of *The Location of Culture* is much more critical than her earlier reading of Bhabha's essays. Essentially, she argues that Bhabha's critique of totalizing theoretical systems can leave us indifferent to the real inequalities constructed and maintained by neocolonialism: this is because only a totalizing system like Marxism has the ambition to explain the global reach of contemporary capitalism.

By contrast, post-structuralism does not aspire to such comprehensive explanation, believing that it can only be symptomatic of philosophical arrogance. Bhabha's work is significantly reliant on the language and ideas of post-structuralism, and so his work is an obvious target for this criticism.

Parry argues that ' "difference" has been diverted by a postmodernist criticism as a theoretical ruse to establish a neutral, ideology-free zone from which the social dissension and political contest inscribed in the antagonist pairing of coloniser/colonised, have been expelled'. (Parry 1994: 15) Further, she complains in much greater detail about the problems that come from locating agency in psychoanalytic processes of ambivalence: 'The effect of moving agency from the subject as insurgent actor to textual performance, is to defuse resistance as practices directed at undermining and defeating an oppressive opponent.' (1994: 16) The spaces of opposition are conflated, and agency becomes conceived as remote from individual or collective experience. Further, this conflation, when extended to relations of metropolis and colony, merely reinforces the lack of attention to real and ongoing inequalities: 'To speak then of metropolis and colony as inhabiting the same in-between, interstitial ground, occludes that this territory was differentially occupied, and that it was contested space, being the site of coercion and resistance, and not of civil negotiation between evenly placed contenders.' (1994: 19) Such an occlusion, Parry ultimately suggests, derives from Bhabha taking his own position as exemplary, that is, he takes his own condition of migrancy as the most general, despite its clear privileges:

> In representing the productive tensions of its own situation as normative and desirable, the privileged post-colonial is prone to denigrate affiliations to class, ethnicity, and emergent nation-state which continue to fashion the self-understanding and energise the resistances of exploited populations in the hinterlands of late imperialism, as well as of immigrant labourers living on the outskirts of one or other metropolis. (1994: 21)

Post-colonial criticism may well derive from an experience of exile which allows writers to think through the complexities of belonging and home. However, this kind of exile is something most readily accessible to privileged academics and literary writers. This is not a problem if their privilege is not identified as representative of the general post-colonial situation: we must remember that not everyone gets to teach at prestigious and well-resourced universities, for example. Unfortunately, sometimes post-colonial criticism loses sight of its own limitations. Post-colonial criticism, from this perspective, is not really that much to do with colonialism, neo-colonialism, or anti-colonialism. It is, rather, the preserve of a privileged few, and its disdain for class and ethnic affiliation is cheaply bought: only when you have some material comfort and stability can you happily give up your attachment to ethnic or national identity. Parry refers to Bhabha's 'translations of an expatriate post-colonial location' (1994: 21), and this phrase seems to be shorthand for her criticism of both his work and post-colonial theory generally: it has been a translation without precautions, or even just a bad translation between languages that needed a lot more care and attention.

That 'exorbitation of discourse' to which Parry refers in her earlier essay seems part of the problem: it is the 'language model', she suggests, that undermines 'Bhabha's many fecund insights into cultural processes'. (1994: 7) In direct response to Parry's review of Bhabha, Iain Chambers writes that Bhabha's work is only one of many textual spaces in which 'the being of language, the being of the West, is not merely contested and deviated, but is forced to speak again in order to reveal its historical provenance, its patriarchal powers, and with them its illusions, its unconscious, its divisions, its limits ... its potential alterity'. (Chambers 1994: 109) As part of his response, Chambers cites various literary writers such as novelist Wilson Harris and poet Derek Walcott, and reminds us that creative language use is not quite as detached from reality as it sometimes seems to be. Regardless, this book has already suggested (particularly in Chapter 2) that to see the 'language model' as a *language* model at all is seriously to misunderstand what is happening whenever that word 'writing' appears in Bhabha's essays.

COLLABORATION: RASHEED ARAEEN

Parry's thoughts about post-colonial theory and its supposed elevation of discourse have none the less had wide-ranging influence. A simple, and forthright, statement of Parry's point is made by Araeen, editor of the art journal *Third Text*, who in 2000 published an article titled 'A New Beginning: Beyond Postcolonial Cultural Theory and Identity Politics'. Its title seems to speak for itself, inviting a rather different way of going about our business than post-colonial theory had envisaged. Post-colonial theory seems equal to, or a synonym for, identity politics, and this has always been a bad thing, somewhat indifferent to the actual inequalities between the post-colonial theorist and those people about whom he or she theorizes. And yet Araeen's article is initially rather respectful of the contribution made by critics like Bhabha, along with Said and Spivak. Indeed, it could be said that he wants art theorists and historians to take responsibility for their own fields: one of his arguments is that these critics, however knowledgeable about visual art they may be, are not specialists, and are supplementing some kind of lack in art history and theory. However, later in the article Araeen becomes more specific in his criticisms, and Bhabha is a major target:

> Since his concept of hybridity and in-between space has created a separate space, specified by the cultural differences of non-white peoples, it has created a separation or dividing line between whites and non-whites; the result is that while white artists can carry on what they always did, appropriating any culture they liked and without carrying with them any sign of their cultural identity, non-white artists must enter the dominant culture by showing their cultural identity cards. (2000: 16)

It is not clear that this scenario follows from Bhabha's understanding of hybridity, but in any case a rather more serious charge is to come. Araeen essentially argues, although not by name, that Bhabha is some kind of native collaborator, a mimic man perhaps:

> Native collaborators have always played an important role in perpetuating colonial power and domination, and it is no different today. They have always occupied the in-between space, to create a buffer between the ruler

and the ruled. The recent globalisation of the capitalist economy, still dominated and controlled by the West, has attained a new power and confidence
which is now being translated through the globalisation of world cultures.
This has created a new space and job opportunities for the neocolonial collaborators. (2000: 17)

Araeen writes as if Bhabha had never heard of Macaulay's infamous
'Minute' on education (1835), or the entire project of creating that
buffer class between the British and Indians; he writes as if the whole
notion of the mimic man was rather flat, undifferentiated, and as if
Bhabha did not recognize his socio-economic situation. But Bhabha
cannot stop being Bhabha, and cannot magically wipe away his familial
and cultural positioning – disclaiming privilege might be merely dishonest. Araeen's position on Bhabha's background provokes him to call
for a revitalized 'Third World' or 'black' art magazine – one that would
reject both of those terms, and related terms, on the basis that those
terms are already exactly what globalization requires, and what it has
already incorporated or even produced. However, Araeen's criticisms,
largely carried out by allusion, seem rather ungenerous in their
implied ascription of motivation. It must be said that his criticisms are
also representative of a certain vein of response to Bhabha's writing.

READING: STUART HALL

A more generous response comes from Stuart Hall, a founding figure
in cultural studies whose interventions in various critical debates over
forty years have always been measured. His understanding of Bhabha
on Fanon is accordingly important, and can be found in *The Fact of
Blackness*, a collection to which Bhabha also contributed. First, Hall
gives some historical overview, and like Parry and Lazarus emphasizes
the question of 'inverting' Fanon's writings; however, Hall writes that
the 'contest over "which text of Fanon's?" as a way of trying to annex
his political legacy after the event is far from concluded'. Hall reminds
us that, whatever some writers might imply, the 'struggle to colonise
Fanon's work has been an on-going process since the moment of his
death'. (Hall 1996: 15) What Hall is getting at is the fact that re-

reading, or remembering, Fanon is not something new, something fashionable contesting the inherent truth of the revolutionary Fanon; remembering Fanon was a process already underway at the moment of, and probably before, his death.

In more specific terms, Hall looks to the fact that so much work was done around, not *The Wretched of the Earth*, but instead *Black Skin, White Masks*, and this of course is where Bhabha comes into the picture. Hall suggests that the process of re-reading Fanon was only made more problematic, and more urgent, by the question of 'how we are to re-read the multi-vocality of *Black Skin, White Masks*'. (1996: 16) Much of Hall's discussion concerns the controversies around Fanon's work, partly derived from the complexity of that one book, and it is unsurprising that it eventually returns to Bhabha's 'Remembering Fanon', the foreword to the reissued text. Hall notes the near-disbelief of critics like Parry, when Bhabha produces his vision of the post-structuralist, quasi-Lacanian Fanon. Yet, Hall suggests, 'his critics, in their haste, do not always acknowledge how clearly Bhabha marks out the points in his text at which his interpretation departs from and goes beyond his Fanonian brief'. (1996: 25) Although Neil Lazarus seems to suggest otherwise, Hall is quite correct here. Even though Lazarus notes Bhabha's references to departure from Fanon, for Lazarus there is still the sense that Bhabha is trying to tell us what Fanon really thought. Hall, by contrast, accepts Bhabha's acknowledgement that he is departing from Fanon in pursuit of contemporary interests, and even implies that what Fanon really thought does not necessarily matter. Hall concisely summarizes Bhabha's reading of Fanon in the following terms:

> It is that Fanon constantly and implicitly poses issues and raises questions in ways which cannot be adequately addressed within the conceptual framework into which he seeks often to resolve them; and that a more satisfactory and complex 'logic' is often implicitly threaded through the interstices of his text, which he does not always follow through but which we can discover by reading him 'against the grain'. In short, Bhabha produces a *symptomatic reading* of Fanon's text. The question for us, then, is whether we should limit such a 'symptomatic reading'? With what authority, but more significantly,

with what effects, do we actively appropriate Fanon's work against the textual grain? (1996: 25)

Unlike Lazarus, then, Hall is sympathetic to Bhabha's reading process, although his open question is to what extent that reading process has any boundaries. Lazarus's argument relies on one assumption: that the truth of Fanon's writings can be traced in their evolution. Of course Lazarus is not relying merely on their consecutive nature, as if the later writings are necessarily more important than the earlier: he would point to the way in which those writings intervene and intersect with other writings and contexts, with the later writings that were much more influential in anti-colonial history. Hall, however, is not quite content with this evolutionary, progressivist picture of Fanon. Hall notes (agreeing, he says, with Benita Parry) that *Black Skin, White Masks* is 'an *open text*, and hence a text we are obliged to go on working *on*, working *with*'. (1996: 34) Bhabha's reading is clearly, for Hall as well as for others, a seminal moment in the ongoing process of remembering Fanon. Although he may not agree with every emphasis in Bhabha's reading of Fanon, Hall is still compelled to ask 'what are we to do with the "uncertain dark" which Bhabha suggests is always the accompaniment to the emergence of truly radical thought?' (1996: 35) When it comes to Fanon, so central a figure in anti-colonial mythology, we have yet to fully deal with being after Bhabha.

POSTCOLONIAL THEORY AS SYMPTOM: HARDT AND NEGRI

If for Hall Bhabha reads Fanon symptomatically, other critics have in turn read Bhabha as a symptom himself. Indeed, although this chapter has focused on narrow responses to Bhabha's work, there are other responses which are much more general, and use Bhabha as emblematic of what is wrong with post-colonialism generally. These responses are very often made in the name of theorizing globalization – to some critics, post-colonialism seems like a distraction from contemporary concerns. Michael Hardt and Antonio Negri's *Empire* (2000) is an influential account of the revolutionary potential of globalization. Rather than settle for examining all the ways in which globalized networks stymie revolutionary change, they argue that everything is in place for a true instantaneity of social change: Marx was right, of course, he was merely lacking the right technology, which he always knew capitalism would relentlessly, remorselessly, and unthinkingly develop. What does this admittedly striking argument have to do with Bhabha's work? Hardt and Negri view various responses to globalization as symptomatic of the transition they see between imperial systems and the total yet dispersive system of empire. Their discussion of post-colonial theory as one symptom of this change is conducted through the example of Bhabha's work.

Importantly, Hardt and Negri see post-colonial theory as almost equivalent to post-modern theory. They see Bhabha's work as 'the clearest and best-articulated example of the continuity between postmodernist and post-colonialist discourses'. (2000: 143) Further, they suggest that 'post-colonial theorists such as Bhabha interest us primarily insofar as they are symptoms of the epochal shift we are undergoing, that is, the passage to Empire'. (2000: 145) This requires some explanation. Because Bhabha's work, like post-colonial theory generally, is concerned with dialectical structures and the analysis of power as self-identical and monolithic, it is an appropriate form of analysis for imperialism. Like post-modernism, post-colonialism mistakenly assumes that the critique of imperialist binaries is effective against the new enemy: their shared emphasis on hybridity is entirely coincident with 'post-modern sovereignty' and the global market, all wishing to liberate differences across boundaries. Post-colonial critique is a useful critique of *modern* sovereignty, but it is 'entirely insufficient for theorizing contemporary global power'. (2000: 146)

Hardt and Negri have an explanation for the popularity of the post-colonial explanatory scheme, and it is an explanation that will be familiar from the earlier discussions of Ahmad, Parry, and Lazarus. However, they make an interesting point, in keeping with the thrust of their book, which is not explicitly present in the other criticisms. They suggest the following:

In our present imperial world, the liberatory potential of the postmodernist and post-colonial discourses that we have described only resonates with the situation of an elite population that enjoys certain rights, a certain level of wealth, and a certain position in the global hierarchy. One should not take this recognition, however, as a complete refutation. It is not really a matter of either/or. Difference, hybridity, and mobility are not liberatory in themselves, but neither are truth, purity, and stasis. The real revolutionary practice refers to the level of *production*. Truth will not make us free, but taking control of the production of truth will. (2000: 156)

Their explanation for post-colonial theory is that it is the world-view of a privileged class position. However, that does not immediately and forever destroy its value. Their further point is that the various categories of thought, whether those of a post-modernism or variations on Marxism, are not in themselves anything without access to production. In other words, there remains a distinction between theory and practice, and any theory that remains at the level of mere theory will also remain inadequate to the tasks of understanding and transforming globalization. Given the general nature of their argument, it is perhaps not surprising that the passages on Bhabha are brief and a little superficial, but their case is still important and has the virtue of taking the philosophical contexts seriously. Bhabha has himself responded to their general charge about the redundancy of the critique of binary oppositions, remarking that 'The aftermath of 9/11 has, I believe, made even more urgent the '80s endeavour to think of issues relating to political and cultural difference beyond the polarities of power and identity.' (MD) In the previous chapter I mentioned Marjorie Perloff arguing that 9/11 demonstrates the inaccuracy of the post-colonial critical perspective. Here, by contrast, Bhabha is arguing that 9/11 shows the *continuing relevance* of that perspective. That *Empire*'s criticism of post-colonial theory closely echoes Perloff's implies, depending on your perspective, either that together they have genuinely isolated the fundamental conceptual problems of that theory, or that neither critical position is fully worked out.

POST-COLONIAL SINGULARITY: HALLWARD

As in the case of Hardt and Negri's book, not all critical responses to Bhabha's work have come from writers hostile to post-structuralism or continental philosophy. Perhaps the most searching and thoughtful response is that of Peter Hallward (2001), who considers post-colonial theory in general and Bhabha in particular to be examples of what he terms a *singularizing* critical tendency. Hallward essentially distinguishes between the singular and the specific, and his argument is that it is only specific critical positions that allow for genuine judgement, in that they do not create their own conditions of judgement but refer to other, external criteria. His position is that post-colonial theory generally creates its own singular plane of immanence, thereby short-circuiting many of the most important issues that are implied by the histories under consideration. Instead of putting its claims to the test of colonial history, post-colonial theory creates its own limited theoretical context.

Hallward's specific points about Bhabha relate to those familiar questions of agency and enunciation that earlier chapters of this book explored. On the question of agency, Hallward notes that Bhabha explicitly asks the question that so many critics demand of him – what does the absolutely prior deconstruction of the sign mean for subjects, agents? (The question is explicitly posed on p. 174 of *The Location of Culture*, among other places.) Bhabha's answer is essentially that those subjects '*incarnate* this indeterminacy pure and simple'. (2001: 24) According to Hallward, then, 'Specific individuals are here always derivative, a result.' (2001: 24) On the inflation of the sign, Hallward goes a step further than the standard criticisms that this chapter has outlined, in line with what he has argued about agency. Other critics point to a textualism, a so-called exorbitation of textuality, but it is none the less possible to imagine an immensely specific and detailed kind of textualist approach. According to Hallward, however, the detail of Bhabha's argument suggests the non-specific: 'Rather than simply treat historical or social situations as linguistic or rhetorical ones, it would be more accurate to say that Bhabha equates creative agency with the precise moment of this differing enunciation as such, the moment "behind" or productive of language itself.' (2001: 25)

Post-colonial agency is a form of creativity, but it is not situated in any real-world situation: instead, it is a condition of any form of expression whatsoever. Behind every utterance there is a possibility of creativity that looks just like post-colonial agency, and indeed is philosophically indistinguishable from it. Accordingly, Hallward argues that this behind-ness operates as an absolute *singularization*: 'Escaping from a situated position relative to other positions, the post-colonial slips between *every* possible position because it refers back, immediately, to that *one* logic that positions every possibility.' (2001: 26) The post-colonial always refers back to a philosophical level, rather than engaging with practical contexts and relations: in fact, post-colonial criticism does not have any necessary connection with the realities of colonialism and neo-colonialism.

From Hallward's perspective, the category of difference in Bhabha licenses a particular kind of de-contextualized theory. It produces the conditions of judgement as a singular plane, within which it is of course impossible to make sense of what actually happens under, say, Apartheid (one of Hallward's examples). This singularized, decontextualized critical perspective produces only the illusion of agency, or of criticism as such, making the categories of the colonial and post-colonial entirely self-serving and self-confirming. If colonialism is all a matter of denying the splitting of agency at the origin, denying the time-lag that makes colonial authority non-identical with itself, then the post-colonial can unobtrusively enter the stage to save the day: 'The colonial enterprise can then be figured as an *inevitably* unsuccessful effort to reduce enunciation to the relation of distinct (i.e. static) identities; the post-colonial enterprise appears, in turn, as the triumphant (and no less inevitable) dissolution of these distinctions through a return to the real process of enunciation.' (2001: 26) Hallward's point is a philosophical version of the question about the level at which Bhabha's work operates; other cultural critics like Terry Eagleton (1998) make this point when they question the sometimes tenuous connection between real-world post-colonialism and academic 'post-colonialism'.

Hallward extends his criticism to cover the question of neo-colonialism, which as you will recall is on the side of the pedagogical or the epistemological, as against the performative or the enunciative. Remember that in Bhabha the pedagogy of the nation insists upon the static, the fixed; however, the truth of enunciation is forever hybrid, distinct from itself, as we know if we refer back to this pre-subjective moment behind everything. Earlier, this non-identical quality is said to be a banality, just the way things are – this position is most fully worked out in the writings of philosopher Alain Badiou, whose work is translated into English by Hallward (see Badiou 2001). Hallward asks, and he is not the first to ask this question, what happens when that fixed-ness, that static quality, remains in place? What do subjects do? Hallward reads Bhabha as implying that such *doing* is simply beside the point, because we are already *done by* language. The subject is, according to Bhabha, just another instance of the prior enunciation; Hallward again: 'It is individuated as *an* enunciation. Since what individuates enunciation is pure *différance*, it is difficult to see how this individuation does anything more than equate any particular individual with an instance of individuation itself.' (2001: 27) In other words, for Hallward all the talk of agency re-entering is just talk – or, and this might come to the same thing, we really should use a different word and accept that this phenomenon is simply not of the same nature as the agency of anti-colonial activists, artists, and writers.

SUMMARY

As this chapter has demonstrated, Bhabha's writing has been the occasion for a significant quantity of more-or-less reasoned debate. Cultural critics agree that his work is foundational in something called post-colonial criticism, but there is a lot of uncertainty about the value of his contribution, or indeed the value of post-colonial studies generally. Much of the criticism accords precisely with the presentation of Bhabha advanced by this book, albeit often with rather different conclusions drawn. It is agreed that Bhabha's reading practice teases out improbable if not impossible positions from the writers he considers, particularly Fanon. Also, it is agreed that his work resists dialectical thinking, and that he wishes to produce distinct modes of historical discourse. Critics like Parry, Lazarus, and Hallward have all challenged these features of Bhabha's work. Not all these critics are what Bhabha might consider 'traditional'. None the less, it seems that many people are arguing past Bhabha, not really taking on his work on the territory it most commonly inhabits. This non-communication is unsurprising, given that Bhabha's work often enough (and necessarily, in his own terms) strays into disciplines in which he is no specialist. He argues strongly for interdisciplinarity, and sometimes the results of this will be marked by omissions that are obvious to the specialist. This non-communication is also why I have concluded with reference to Peter Hallward's work, for the questions he raises in relation to Bhabha's work operate in the same terms, take these terms seriously, and yet still fundamentally question Bhabha's thinking: the question Hallward raises, particularly in relation to ethics, may well turn out to be (as he says) one of the biggest contemporary philosophical questions, and it would not be surprising if Bhabha had further contributions to make.

FURTHER READING

TEXTS BY BHABHA

A comprehensive bibliography of Bhabha's work can be found online at the Center for Critical Theory, University of California, Irvine. You will see just how often and in how many different places Bhabha's essays have been reprinted. The bibliography I give here refers to texts I have discussed in this book, and other important essays that are not included in *The Location of Culture*. However, I have also included earlier versions of essays from that book, some of which are sufficiently different (and are perhaps more accessible) to be considered separately. The comments offered introduce the texts in question, and also often include directions to sections of this book.

1983

'The Other Question ... , *Screen* (November–December 1983), 24(6), 18–36.
This important early essay appears in various forms over the years; the definitive version appears in *The Location of Culture*, but this one is an easier read. In this essay, Bhabha considers how Said's sense of discourse is uni-directional; he is, therefore, outlining arguably the

central point of his work, that colonial discourse is ambivalent, divided at its point of enunciation.

1986

'Foreword: Remembering Fanon: Self, Psyche, and the Colonial Condition.' Introduction to Frantz Fanon's *Black Skin, White Masks*, London and Sydney: Pluto Press, pp. vii–xxvi.

This is perhaps the single most important work in the 1980s reconsideration of Fanon's work, for good or ill. Again, revised versions of this essay appear elsewhere, but this one is accessible and has the useful bonus of coming with the work it discusses, allowing you to decide for yourself just how viable a reading it is.

1989

'At the Limits', *Artforum* (May 1989), 27(9),11–12.

This essay looks at the events surrounding Salman Rushdie's *The Satanic Verses*, giving a sense of the precariousness of hybridity and cultural translation.

1990

(ed.) *Nation and Narration*, London: Routledge.

1.   Homi K. Bhabha. Introduction: Narrating the Nation: 1–7.
2.   Ernest Renan. What is a Nation? 8–22.
3.   Martin Thom. Tribes within Nations: The Ancient Germans and the History of Modern France: 23–43.
4.   Timothy Brennan. The National Longing for Form: 44–70.
5.   Doris Sommer. Irresistible Romance: The Foundational Fictions of Latin America: 71–98.
6.   Sneja Gunew. Denaturalizing Cultural Nationalisms: Multicultural Readings of 'Australia': 99–120.
7.   Geoffrey Bennington. Postal Politics and the Institution of the Nation: 121–37.

8.   Simon During. Literature – Nationalism's Other? The Case for Revision: 138–53.

9.   John Barrell. Sir Joshua Reynolds and the Englishness of English Art: 154–76.

10.   David Simpson. Destiny Made Manifest: The Styles of Whitman's Poetry: 177–96.

11.   Rachel Bowlby. Breakfast in America: Uncle Tom's Cultural Histories: 197–212.

12.   Bruce Robbins. Telescopic Philanthropy: Professionalism and Responsibility in *Bleak House*: 213–30.

13.   James Snead. European Pedigrees/African Contagions: Nationality, Narrative, and Communality in Tutuola, Achebe, and Reed: 231–49.

14.   Francis Mulhern. English Reading: 250–64.

15.   Gillian Beer. The Island and the Aeroplane: The Case of Virginia Woolf: 265–90.

16.   Homi K. Bhabha. DissemiNation: Time, Narrative, and the Margins of the Modern Nation: 291–322.

This is a wide-ranging collection of essays, book-ended by Bhabha's contributions which are his classic statements on national narratives. 'DissemiNation' appears in essentially the same form as in *The Location of Culture*. The other essays are by writers of various theoretical persuasions, some of whom are much closer to Bhabha than others; all of the essays are interesting and specific theoretical considerations of the nation. The Renan essay, 'What is a Nation?', is an important historical resource.

1991

a. 'The Third Space: Interview with Homi K. Bhabha', in Jonathan Rutherford (ed.) *Identity: Community, Culture, Difference*, London: Lawrence & Wishart, pp. 207–21.

This interview is an accessible and short introduction to Bhabha's sense of identity in process; as with his other interviews, this can be a more accessible way into his ideas than his essays.

b. 'Threatening Pleasures', *Sight and Sound* (N.S.) (August), 1(4), 17–19.

This is a discussion of Isaac Julien's film *Young Soul Rebels*, with Stuart Hall and Paul Gilroy. This interview is accessible, and a good opportunity to read three central post-colonial critics playing off one another. A sense of the necessarily negotiated nature of communal identity comes through strongly.

c. 'Art and National Identity: A Critics' Symposium', *Art in America* (September), 79(9), 82.

Here Bhabha outlines the post-colonial challenge to liberal notions of national identity, particularly emphasizing the importance of dissensus. As opposed to a celebratory hybridity, Bhabha elaborates the inherently risky business of cultural hybridization.

d. ' "Caliban Speaks to Prospero": Cultural Identity and the Crisis of Representation', in Philomena Marini (ed.) *Critical Fictions: the Politics of Imaginative Writing*, Seattle: Bay Press, pp. 62–5.

Brief outline of a post-colonial or minoritarian perspective, particularly in the context of the contemporary novel.

1992

a. 'The World and the Home', *Social Text* (1992), 10(31–2), 141–53.

Later revised for 'Locations of Culture' in *The Location of Culture*, this essay is an important set of readings of the uncanny in literature, looking at novelists from Henry James to Nadine Gordimer. The reading of Toni Morrison's *Beloved* forms an important part of 'Locations of Culture'.

b. 'Postcolonial Authority and Postmodern Guilt', in Lawrence Grossberg, Cary Nelso, and Paula A. Treichler (eds) *Cultural Studies*, New York and London: Routledge, pp. 56–68.

Some familiar arguments about how the post-colonial rewrites the post-modern are made accessible in this talk. Much of this reappears as 'The Postcolonial and the Postmodern' in *The Location of Culture*, but is more accessible in this form. Additionally, the following audience discussion features useful questions and answers, including comments about Bhabha's difficulty.

c. 'Postcolonial Criticism', in Stephen Greenblatt and Giles Gunn (eds) *Redrawing the Boundaries: The Transformation of English and American Literary Studies*, New York: MLA, pp. 437–65.

This essay is a clear statement of the post-colonial theoretical project, outlining its transnational and translational aspects. It gives a sense of how literary constructions might be central to the study of constructed cultures and traditions.

d. 'Double Visions', *Artforum* (January), 30(5), 85–9. Review of the exhibition of the same name, marking five hundred years since Columbus's 'discoveries'. Bhabha pays particular attention to the implied notion of time structuring its 'marvellous parallelism'.

1994

a. *The Location of Culture*, London: Routledge.

1.	The Commitment to Theory: 19–39.
2.	Interrogating Identity: Frantz Fanon and the Postcolonial Prerogative: 40–65.
3.	The Other Question: Stereotype, Discrimination and the Discourse of Colonialism: 66–84.
4.	Of Mimicry and Man: The Ambivalence of Colonial Discourse: 85–92.
5.	Sly Civility: 93–101.
6.	Signs Taken for Wonders: Questions of Ambivalence and Authority under a Tree outside Delhi, May 1817: 102–22.
7.	Articulating the Archaic: Cultural Difference and Colonial Nonsense: 123–38.
8.	DissemiNation: Time, Narrative and the Margins of the Modern Nation: 139–70.
9.	The Postcolonial and the Postmodern: The Question of Agency: 171–97.
10.	By Bread Alone: Signs of Violence in the Mid-Nineteenth Century: 198–211.
11.	How Newness Enters the World: Postmodern Space, Postcolonial Times and the Trials of Cultural Translation: 212–35.

12. Conclusion: 'Race', Time and the Revision of Modernity: 236–75.

The central text when reading Bhabha. It is difficult to choose any specific essays as more important than others, and you should really try all of them. However, the Introduction and Chapter one are relatively accessible. Some of the other essays are more straightforward in their earlier versions, here being more poetic; that poetry, however, is part of the rewarding experience of reading his work.

b. 'Anxious Nations, Nervous States', in Joan Copjec (ed.) *Supposing the Subject*, London: Verso, pp. 201–17.

This essay examines the question of the nation again, and forms an important supplement to 'DissemiNation'. Here Bhabha translates his thinking of the pedagogical/performative pairing into psychoanalytic terms, writing of the paranoia of official national narratives.

1995

a. 'In a Spirit of Calm Violence', in Gyan Prakash (ed.) *After Colonialism: Imperial Histories and Postcolonial Displacements*, Princeton: Princeton University Press, pp. 326–44.

Bhabha focuses on Foucault and the uncanny in this article, much of which is familiar from comparative discussion of post-modernism and post-colonialism in *The Location of Culture*.

b. 'Black and White and Read All Over', *Artforum* (October), 34(2), 16–17, 114, 116.

Discusses and defends the so-called New Black Public intellectuals, paying particular attention to their hybridized positions, and casting a backward glance to James Baldwin in explanation of their difficulties.

c. 'Dance This Diss Around', *Artforum* (April), 33(8), 19–20.

A suggestive analysis of 'victim art', beginning with Sylvia Plath's 'Lady Lazarus' and moving on to Bill T. Jones's *Still/Here*, which was performed by HIV-positive dancers. Bhabha examines the reasons critics have refused to interpret these artworks, and reads them as instances of survival and negotiation.

d. ' "Black Male": The Whitney Museum of American Art', *Artforum* (February), 33(6), 86–87, 110.

Again, here Bhabha begins with a specific exhibition, of representations of 'the' black male, and writes around it to produce the beginnings of a counter-stereotypical representative vision. Like many of his writings for *Artforum*, the context and conversational manner make this piece accessible.

e. 'Translator Translated: W. J. T. Mitchell talks with Homi Bhabha', *Artforum* (March) 33(7), 80–3, 110, 114, 118–19.

Mitchell's interview is an excellent introduction to Bhabha's life and work, featuring lengthy comments about Parsi identity, defence of his work's difficulty, and revealing discussion of the role of theory and interdisciplinarity.

1996

a. 'Day by Day ... With Frantz Fanon', in Alan Read (ed.) *The Fact of Blackness: Frantz Fanon and Visual Representation*, Seattle: Bay Press, pp. 186–205.

Later discussion of Fanon, which is particularly important because 'Remembering Fanon' has been so controversial in recent discussions of his life and work. Bhabha looks in depth at Fanon's methods, and their implied notion of time.

b. 'Aura and Agora: On Negotiating Rapture and Speaking Between', in Richard Francis (ed.) *Negotiating Rapture. The Power of Art to Transform Lives*, Chicago: Museum of Contemporary Art, pp. 8–16.

Written for the catalogue of the 1996 exhibition *Negotiating Rapture*, Bhabha uses painting and poetry to pursue the meaning of negotiation, emphasizing its quality of mediation without presumed consensus.

c. 'Unpacking my library ... again', in Iain Chambers and Lydia Curti (eds) *The Postcolonial Question*, London: Routledge, pp. 199–211.

This essay presents further thoughts on the subject in process, history, and memory, deriving from Walter Benjamin and Adrienne Rich; it also includes important gestures in the direction of 'vernacular cosmopolitanism'. The essay is part of Bhabha's work-in-progress on cosmopolitanism.

d. 'Rethinking Authority: Interview with Homi K. Bhabha', *Angelaki*, 2(2), 59–63.

Short and extremely accessible talk with cultural studies specialists, especially covering the importance of the post-colonial perspective for cultural studies.

e. 'Laughing Stock', *Artforum* (October), 35(2), 15–16, 132.

Interesting discussion of the controversy surrounding the journal *Social Text*, which published a hoax article by physicist Alan Sokal; Sokal revealed his hoax, and argued that he wanted to defend truth from post-modern relativism. Bhabha explores the unconscious structures of Sokal's text, and so gives a sense of his own notion of truth.

1997

a. 'Queen's English', *Artforum* (March), 35(7), 25–6, 107.

Drawing on speech act theory and Roland Barthes's idea of idiolects, Bhabha here considers Ebonics, also known as African American Vernacular English (AAVE), as one instance of vernacularization and hybridized speech.

b. 'Editor's Introduction: Minority Maneuvers and Unsettled Negotiations', *Critical Inquiry* (Spring), 23(3), 431–59.

An introduction to a special issue of the influential interdisciplinary journal, covering familiar issues of the minoritarian, the hybrid, and processes of negotiation.

c. 'Designer Creations', *Artforum* (December), 36(4), 11–12, 14, 130.

This essay sets off from a brief discussion of Gianni Versace and Diana, Princess of Wales. It explores Claude Lefort's notion of the *entre-nous* in relation to mass media. Reprinted in Mandy Merck (ed.) (1998) *After Diana: Irreverent Elegies*, London: Verso, pp. 103–10.

d. ' "Fireflies Caught in Molasses": Questions of Cultural Translation', in Rosalind Krauss *et al.* (eds) *October: The Second Decade, 1986–1996*, Cambridge, MA: MIT Press, pp. 211–22.

This essay is a further example of Bhabha's reading of literature, featuring a particularly interesting consideration of Derek Walcott's poetry. Bhabha directs this reading towards a consideration of post-colonial temporal disjunction; familiarly, the post-colonial revises modernity, producing the retroactive ghostly presence of slavery, for example.

e. 'Postscript: Bombs Away in Front-Line Suburbia', in Roger Silverstone (ed.) *Visions of Suburbia*, London: Routledge, pp. 298–303.

This brief essay looks at the connection between suburbia and conservative values in the US. Bhabha suggests that a certain imagined community defines itself through negative definition, being clearly against things like political correctness. He describes this self-definition as evidence of a 'national paranoia', which draws the boundaries between the acceptable and unacceptable all too clearly.

f. 'Liberalism's Sacred Cow', accessed at http://bostonreview.net/BR22.5/bhabha.html on 22 June 2004.

Here Bhabha responds to Susan Moller Okin's question, 'Is multiculturalism bad for women?' (see Okin 1997). Okin suggests that feminism and multiculturalism might well come into conflict. Bhabha responds that it is not easy to divide minority and majority cultures into non-liberal (perhaps even illiberal) and liberal, and that discussions of minority cultures often imply a fixed idea of both minority and majority. Okin implies that there are fixed cultures, and that these cultures are best judged in terms of conflict, a position to which Bhabha cannot subscribe.

g. 'Re-Inventing Britain: A Manifesto', *British Studies Now* 9 (April), 9–10.

This accessible proposal outlines a conference focusing on art and cultural theory that moves on from traditional multiculturalism's stress on identity. Bhabha signals the importance of hybridity and cosmopolitanism for his proposal, as you might expect, but also places emphasis on *secularism* – one question being, are liberal secular cultures the best forum for discussion in a multicultural global context?

h. 'Halfway House', *Artforum* 35.9, 11–13.

In this short and accessible piece, Bhabha further develops the idea that home is not simply a place of safety and comfort, but is also a place of disorientation and internal division – importantly, this experience can be productive. As examples, Bhabha discusses suggestive moments in Toni Morrison's work.

1998

a. 'On the Irremovable Strangeness of Being Different', *PMLA* 113(1), 34–9.

This is a short discussion of the mutual imbrication of apparently opposed sites of difference: the bazaar and the gentleman's club. It implies various counter-arguments to any polarizing perspective on contemporary events. It also briefly discusses Forster's *A Passage to India*.

b. 'Culture's In Between', in David Bennett (ed.) *Multicultural States: Rethinking difference and identity*, London: Routledge, pp. 29–47.

This is an important essay that foregrounds Bhabha's emphasis on cultural rights, including an early discussion of philosopher Charles Taylor on *partial milieux*. Accessible points are made linking the idea of hybridity with issues around cultural rights, and so the essay is an explicit bridge between the work collected in *The Location of Culture* and more recent writing.

c. 'Anish Kapoor: Making Emptiness', in *Anish Kapoor*, London: Hayward Gallery, pp. 11–41.

This is an interesting essay on the ethics implied by this artist's work, including discussion of philosopher Emmanuel Lévinas.

d. 'Joking Aside: The Idea of a Self-Critical Community', in Bryan Cheyette and Laura Marcus (eds) *Modernity, Culture and 'the Jew'*, Cambridge: Polity Press, pp. xv–xx.

An arresting if counter-intuitive investigation of the joke as a minority speech-act, working to unfreeze stereotypes and re-start the circulation of cultural representations.

e. 'The White Stuff', *Artforum* (May), 36(9), 21–2, 24.

This discussion of whiteness studies gives a good sense of how Bhabha's thought relates to contemporary discourses on race and ethnicity.

1999

a. 'Miniaturizing Modernity: Shahzia Sikander in Conversation with Homi K. Bhabha', *Public Culture: Bulletin of the Project for Transnational Cultural Studies* (Winter), 11(1), 146–51.

This is an edited version of Bhabha's discussion with Sikander, which took place when Chicago University exhibited Sikander's work in 1998. Bhabha is interested in hybridity within an apparently monolithic 'Eastern' culture, something brought out by Sikander's work.

b. 'Arrivals and departures', in Hamid Naficy (ed.) *Home, Exile, Homeland: Film, Media, and the Politics of Place*, London: Routledge, pp. vii–xii.

A foreword to an edited collection, this essay considers how virtual communities might either reproduce or challenge the temporal structures of the nation-state. This interesting text discusses the internet, fundamentalism, nationalism, and the minoritarian in ways that will be suggestive for some time.

c. 'For Edward Said: On the 20th Anniversary of *Orientalism*', *Emergences* 9(1), 9–10.

This poem marked the anniversary of *Orientalism*'s publication, thematizing and enacting the complex movements of aesthetics and politics evident throughout Said's work and often the object of Bhabha's own writings.

2000

a. 'On Minorities: Cultural Rights', *Radical Philosophy* 100 (March/April), 3–6.

This is a brief but clear discussion of cultural rights, particularly the continued bias towards the rights of national communities. The basic arguments follow on from 'Culture's In Between', and are given more detail in the Amnesty Lecture (2003).

b. 'Surviving Theory: A Conversation with Homi K. Bhabha', in Fawzia Afzal-Khan and Kalpana Seshadri-Crooks (eds) *The Pre-Occupation of Postcolonial Studies*, Durham, NC and London: Duke University Press, pp. 369–79.

A good introductory talk, which enlightens the interviewer as well as the reader: it's good to remember that not only students find Bhabha challenging reading.

c. 'On Cultural Choice', in Marjorie Garber, Beatrice Hanssen and

Rebecca L. Walkowitz (eds) *The Turn to Ethics*, New York and London: Routledge, pp. 181–200.

This paper considers the joke again, but also connects this discussion with Bhabha's thoughts on cultural rights. This is a useful place to see how his apparently disparate recent work has coherence.
d. 'The Right to Narrate', accessed at http://www.uchicago.edu/docs/millennium/bhabha/bhabha—a.html on 5 December 2003.
Further development of Bhabha's emphasis on the right to narrate, referring not only to literary narrations but also to a more general right for self-representation and recognition. He draws together ideas of interpretative community and cosmopolitanism, suggesting again the need for uncertain and precarious translation in pursuit of the ideal if necessarily open communal horizon.
e. 'Cosmopolitanisms' (with Carol A. Breckenridge, Sheldon Pollock and Dipesh Chakrabarty), *Public Culture* 12(3) (Fall), 577–89.
This essay introduces a special issue of *Public Culture* on cosmopolitanism. Cosmopolitanism is seen as something always still to come, which must necessarily remain open. Instead of being one form of paradoxically Eurocentric universalism, cosmopolitanism is imagined as necessarily plural – and for this, feminism is put forward as a model. Universalism must be situated, in other words it must be vernacular.

2002

'Foreword' to Dipesh Chakrabarty, *Habitations of Modernity: Essays in the Wake of Subaltern Studies*, Chicago: Chicago University Press, pp. ix–xiii.
Brief reflections on Chakrabarty's book, beginning with comments on what it means to read a text *as a friend*, moving on to discuss historical narratives that exceed nation-states. Bhabha is specifically interested in Chakrabarty's elaborations of subaltern agency, and fragmentary subaltern experiences of history and citizenship.

2003

a. 'Democracy De-realized', *Diogenes* 50(1), 27–35.

An essay on the post-9/11 world, drawing on earlier arguments and other work in progress to criticize the discourse of civilizational clash.

b. 'On Writing Rights', in Matthew J. Gibney (ed.) *Globalizing Rights: the Oxford Amnesty Lectures 1999*, Oxford: Oxford University Press, pp. 162–83.

This is a significant statement of Bhabha's position on human rights discourse, drawing on many arguments and examples with which you will be familiar from earlier essays. If you want to see the direction in which Bhabha's work is heading, this essay is a good choice.

c. 'Making difference: Homi K. Bhabha on the legacy of the culture wars', *Artforum* (April), accessed at http://www.findarticles.com/cf—dls/m0268/8—41/101938552/p1/article.jhtml on 5 December 2003.

Reflections on identity politics in the 1980s, with Bhabha paying close attention to minoritarian forms of identification and affiliation, leading to 'difference in equality'. Bhabha argues against the dismissal of post-modernism, etc., as merely cultural logics of late capitalism.

2005

'Adagio', *Critical Inquiry* 31 (Winter), 371–80.

Here Bhabha reflects on the legacy of Edward Said, writing of the *speed* of thought: how fast should we think, how fast should critical reflection move? Looking particularly at Said's *After the Last Sky*, Bhabha insists on the importance of *slowness*. This journal issue is devoted to Said's work, and also contains Bhabha interviewing Noam Chomsky.

WORKS DISCUSSING BHABHA

Ahmad, Aijaz (1995) 'The politics of literary postcoloniality', *Race and Class* 36(3), 1–20.

Ahmad's position on post-colonial theory is the clearest criticism of the field; here he discusses Bhabha in particular, and also Robert Young, as exemplifying the faults of post-colonial theory.

Chambers, Iain (1994) 'Exposure, abeyance and dislocation: Some comments on Benita Parry's discussion of Homi Bhabha's *The Location of Culture*', *Third Text* 31, 108–10.

Chambers responds in brief and accessible fashion to one particular critic of Bhabha, but his comments have general relevance.

Childs, Peter, and Patrick Williams (1996) 'Bhabha's hybridity', in *An Introduction to Post-colonial Theory*, London: Prentice Hall, pp. 122–56.

This chapter, in a general introduction to post-colonial theory, is a concise and fair explanation of Bhabha's main themes.

Eakin, Emily (2001) 'Homi Bhabha: Harvard's Prize Catch', *New York Times* 17 November.

If you want to get a sense of the controversy surrounding Bhabha as an individual, rather than his work, this article is a good place to start.

Easthope, Antony (1998) 'Bhabha, hybridity and identity', *Textual Practice* 12(2), 341–8.

This is an extremely focused and detailed reading of Bhabha's apparent obsession with hybridity, which also criticizes Derrida; it is slightly misleading in its readings of Bhabha and in particular of Derrida, but none the less is a clear statement of objections towards one view of hybridity.

Evaristo, Bernardine *et al.* (1999) 'Reinventing Britain: a forum', *Wasafiri* 29 (Spring), 49.

Commentary on Bhabha's manifesto for 'Reinventing Britain'. This is a short, witty, and accessible objection from a cultural practitioner, not just to Bhabha, but also to cultural theory generally.

Gates, Henry Louis, Jr (1991) 'Critical Fanonism', *Critical Inquiry* 17 (Spring), 457–70.

Gates provides a detailed and theoretically informed overview of 1980s re-readings of Fanon, which inevitably spends some time on Bhabha's own reading. This essay is interesting as a sympathetic perspective on Bhabha's reading practice.

Gewertz, Ken (2002) 'Telling tales out of, and in, class', *Harvard University Gazette*, 31 January.

This article gives further important biographical information, and some accessible statements of Bhabha's ideas.

Giroux, Henry A., and Susan Searls Giroux (2000) 'Teaching the Political with Homi Bhabha', in Henry A. Giroux, *Impure Acts: The Practical Politics of Cultural Studies*, London: Routledge.

This chapter looks specifically at Bhabha's ideas on pedagogy, exploring their openings and limitations. The basic question asked is, how does the performative function pedagogically? The conclusion is that Bhabha's strategies must be supplemented if they are to lead to practical transformations.

Hall, Stuart (1996) 'The After-life of Frantz Fanon: Why Fanon? Why Now? Why *Black Skin, White Masks?*', in Alan Read (ed.) *The Fact of Blackness: Frantz Fanon and Visual Representation*, Seattle: Bay Press, pp. 12–37.

This essay looks at the reasons for renewed attention to Fanon's work, and gives a detailed reading of Bhabha on Fanon. In particular, because he thinks Fanon's text is open to various interpretations, Hall is sympathetic to Bhabha's reading methods.

Hallward, Peter (2001) *Absolutely Post-Colonial: Writing Between the Singular and the Specific*, Manchester: Manchester University Press.

Hallward reads Bhabha as a clear example of a singularizing tendency in post-colonial theory. This means that post-colonial theory – with concepts like hybridity – operates on terms of its own creation, as opposed to more politically committed, relational or specific forms of criticism. You could see this as an argument against cultural relativism: post-colonial theory, on this view, does not provide us with any tools for judgement or genuine criticism.

Hardt, Michael, and Antonio Negri (2000) *Empire*, Cambridge MA: Harvard University Press.

Hardt and Negri discuss Bhabha as an example of critical work suitable for the age of imperialism, but no longer appropriate in an age of post-modern empire. They see his work as symptomatic of the inability to come to terms with the radically new qualities of empire – a word which roughly refers to what is more often called globalization.

Larsen, Neil (2000) 'DetermiNation: Postcolonialism, Poststructuralism, and the Problem of Ideology', in Fawzia Afzal-Khan and Kalpana

Seshadri-Crooks (eds) *The Pre-Occupation of Postcolonial Studies*, Durham, NC and London: Duke University Press, pp. 141–56.

Larsen develops Aijaz Ahmad's criticisms of post-colonial theory, discussing Spivak but focusing on Bhabha's work in particular. Larsen suggests that Bhabha is aware of potential objections to his work, producing ever more minute conceptual distinctions in anticipation of criticism. This is the most comprehensive statement of the argument that post-colonial theory is an ideology.

Lazarus, Neil (1999) *Nationalism and Cultural Practice in the Postcolonial World*, Cambridge: Cambridge University Press.

Lazarus, like Benita Parry, is concerned to challenge Bhabha's apparent dismissal of nationalism. This book contains a lengthy critical reading of Bhabha's interpretation of Fanon, which argues that Bhabha tends to warp Fanon's meaning.

Moore-Gilbert, Bart (1996) ' "The Bhabhal of Tongues": Reading Kipling, reading Bhabha', in Bart Moore-Gilbert (ed.) *Writing India 1757–1990*, Manchester: Manchester University Press, pp. 111–38.

Moore-Gilbert reads Kipling through Bhabha's work, emphasizing the ambivalence of colonial authority in Kipling's stories. Moore-Gilbert uses Bhabha to challenge earlier readings of Kipling, which saw his writing as monological. At the same time, Moore-Gilbert uses Kipling to explore the limitations of Bhabha's methods, particularly their lack of concern for colonialism's violent effectiveness.

—— (1997) *Postcolonial Theory: Contexts, Practices, Politics*, London: Verso.

Like Young's *White Mythologies*, this book positions Bhabha in relation to Said and Spivak. Moore-Gilbert also brings other contexts and comparisons into play, particularly drawing out points of contact between Bhabha and Wilson Harris. None the less, in the final analysis Bhabha's coherence is questioned.

Papastergiadis, Nicos (1996) 'Ambivalence in Cultural Theory: Reading Homi Bhabha's *Dissemi-Nation*', in J. C. Hawley (ed.) *Writing the Nation*, Amsterdam: Rodopi, pp. 176–93.

This is a detailed examination of Bhabha's understanding of the ambivalence governing all national narrative. Papastergiadis also defends the use of *hybridity* as a term, in spite of its negative historical uses.

Parry, Benita (1987) 'Problems in Current Theories of Colonial Discourse', *Oxford Literary Review* 9(1–2), 27–58.

An early statement of Benita Parry's problems with post-colonial theory, looking particularly at Spivak and Bhabha. Interestingly, even though Spivak is the self-avowed Marxist, at this point Parry is more sympathetic towards Bhabha. Like 'Signs of Our Times', this essay is reprinted in Parry, *Postcolonial Studies: A Materialist Critique* (London: Routledge, 1994), pp. 13–36.

—— (1994) 'Signs of Our Times: Discussion of Homi Bhabha's *The Location of Culture*', *Third Text* 38/39, 5–24.

This is probably the most detailed response to Bhabha's work (up to 1994), giving clear and well-referenced explanations of Parry's problems with his ideas. Like 'Problems in Current Theories of Colonial Discourse', this essay is reprinted in Parry, *Postcolonial Studies: A Materialist Critique* (London: Routledge, 1994), pp. 55–74.

Perloff, Marjorie (1998) 'Cultural Liminality/Aesthetic Closure?: the 'Interstitial Perspective' of Homi Bhabha', accessed at http://www.buffalo.edu/epc/authors/perloff/bhabha.html on 20 March 2002.

Perloff offers a close reading of Goethe and Bakhtin, used by Bhabha as examples in his discussion of holistic national narratives. Perloff makes a persuasive case that Bhabha's readings neglect the specific nature of literary texts and other artworks. In important ways, she argues, Goethe and Bakhtin are hybrid, whatever Bhabha argues.

Pickering, Michael (2001) *Stereotyping: the Politics of Representation*, London: Palgrave.

As part of his general study of stereotypes, Pickering offers a thorough criticism of Bhabha's reliance on an apparently ahistorical psychoanalysis. Pickering's analysis criticizes Bhabha's 'textualism', suggesting that this emphasis leads to an unrealistically unified understanding of colonial stereotyping.

Sakamoto, Rumi (1996) 'Japan, Hybridity and the Creation of

Colonialist Discourse', *Theory, Culture & Society: Explorations in Critical Social Science* 13(3),113–28.

Sakamoto argues that Yukichi Fukuzawa, a scholar of 'Western learning' in Tokugawa Japan, theorized a hybrid Japan that moved beyond the dichotomy of Japan–the West, only to create a new dichotomy, Japan–Asia. She suggests that Bhabha's theory of hybridity neglects the possibility of such a substitution.

Young, Robert (1990) *White Mythologies: Writing History and the West*, London: Routledge.

This book inserts Bhabha into a lineage of writers critical of Marxist Eurocentrism. One chapter focuses on Bhabha's early work, looking at its potential and problems in great detail. The second edition (2004) has a preface by Bhabha.

—— (1995) *Colonial Desire: Hybridity in Theory, Culture and Race*, London: Routledge.

Whilst seeing Bhabha as one of the 'Holy Trinity' of post-colonial studies, this book interrogates the idea of hybridity, investigating the ways its use in contemporary cultural theory often seems to repeat nineteenth-century colonial discourses.

—— (2001) *Postcolonialism: An historical introduction*, Oxford: Blackwell.

Here Young positions Bhabha in a wide-ranging comparative study of post-colonialism as historical phenomenon – or really, a set of related, often conflicting, phenomena, which he opts to call *Tricontinentalism*.

WORKS CITED

For bibliographic information on works by Bhabha, see pp. 171–83 in Further reading.

Achebe, Chinua (1958 [2001]) *Things Fall Apart*, London: Penguin.

—— (1977 [1997]) 'An Image of Africa: Racism in Conrad's "Heart of Darkness" ', in Bart Moore-Gilbert, Gareth Stanton and Willy Maley (eds) *Postcolonial Criticism*, London: Longman, pp. 112–25.

Ahmad, Aijaz (1992) *In Theory: Classes, Nations, Literatures*, London: Verso.

Anderson, Benedict (1991) *Imagined Communities: Reflections on the Origin and Spread of Nationalism*, London: Verso.

Apple, Michael W. (1996) *Cultural Politics and Education*, Buckingham: Open University Press.

Araeen, Rasheed (2000) 'A New Beginning: Beyond Postcolonial Cultural Theory and Identity Politics', *Third Text* 50 (Spring), 3–20.

Arendt, Hannah (1951) *The Origins of Totalitarianism*, New York: Harcourt Brace.

—— (1958) *The Human Condition*, Chicago: Chicago University Press.

Badiou, Alain (2001) *Ethics: An Essay on the Understanding of Evil*, trans. Peter Hallward, London: Verso.

Bakhtin, M. M. (1986) *Speech Genres and Other Late Essays*, trans. Vern W. McGee, Austin: University of Texas Press.

Baldick, Chris (1983) *The Social Mission of English Criticism: 1848–1932*, Oxford: Clarendon Press.

Bhattacharyya, Gargi (1991) 'Cultural Education in Britain: From the Newbolt Report to the National Curriculum', *Oxford Literary Review* 13(1–2), 4–19.

Boehmer, Elleke (1998) 'Post-Colonial Literary Studies: A Neo-Orientalism?', in C. C. Barfoot and Theo d'Haen (eds) *Oriental Prospects: Western Literature and the Lure of the East*, Amsterdam: Rodopi, pp. 241–56.

Brennan, Timothy (2001) 'World Music Does Not Exist', *Discourse* 23 (1) (Winter), 44–62.

Butler, Judith (1997) *The Psychic Life of Power*, Stanford: Stanford University Press.

Carey, Peter (2003) *My Life as a Fake*, London: Faber and Faber.

Césaire, Aimé (1939 [2001]) *Notebook of a Return to the Native Land*, trans. A. Smith and C. Eshleman, Middletown CT: Wesleyan University Press.

Chaudhuri, Amit (2004) 'In the Waiting-Room of History', *London Review of Books* 27 (12) (24 June), 3, 5–6, 8.

Clifford, James (1997) *Routes*, Cambridge MA: Harvard University Press.

Conrad, Joseph (1899 [1973]) *Heart of Darkness*, London: Penguin.

Coombes, Anne E. (1994) 'The Recalcitrant Object: Culture Contact and the Question of Hybridity', in Francis Barker *et al.* (eds) *Colonial Discourse / Postcolonial Theory*, Manchester: Manchester University Press, pp. 89–114.

Deitcher, David *et al.* (2000) *The Film Art of Isaac Julien*, New York: Center for Curatorial Studies.

Derrida, Jacques (1976) *Of Grammatology*, trans. G. C. Spivak, Baltimore: Johns Hopkins University Press.

—— (1978) *Writing and Difference*, trans. A. Bass, Chicago: Chicago University Press.

—— (1987) *The Post Card: From Socrates to Freud and Beyond*, trans. A. Bass, Chicago: Chicago University Press.

—— (1994) *Specters of Marx: The State of the Debt, the Work of Mourning, and the New International*, trans. P. Kamuf, London: Routledge.

—— (1996) *Archive Fever*, trans. E. Prenowitz, Stanford: Stanford University Press.

—— (1997) *Politics of Friendship*, trans. G. Collins, London: Verso.

Dirlik, Arif (1994) 'The Postcolonial Aura: Third World Criticism in the Age of Global Capitalism', *Critical Inquiry* 20 (Winter), 328–56.

Douzinas, Costas (2001) 'Human Rights, Humanism, and Desire', *Angelaki* 6(3) (December), 183–206.

Du Bois, W. E. B. (1995) *W. E. B. Du Bois: A Reader*, New York: Henry Holt & Company.

Eagleton, Terry (1998) 'Postcolonialism and "Postcolonialism" ', *Interventions* 1(1), 24–6.

Fanon, Frantz (1952 [1986]) *Black Skin, White Masks*, trans. C. L. Markmann, London: Pluto Press.

—— (1961 [1967]) *The Wretched of the Earth*, trans. C. Farrington, London: Penguin.

—— (1970) *Toward the African Revolution: Political Essays,* trans. H. Chevalier, New York: Grove Press.

—— (1988) *A Dying Colonialism*, trans. H. Chevalier, New York: Grove Press.

Forster, E. M. (1924) *A Passage to India*, London: Hogarth Press.

Foucault, Michel (1965) *Madness and Civilization*, trans. R. Howard, New York: Pantheon.

—— (1970) *The Order of Things. An Archaeology of the Human Sciences*, trans. A. S. Smith, London: Tavistock.

—— (1972) *The Archaeology of Knowledge*, trans. A. S. Smith, London: Tavistock.

—— (1973) *The Birth of the Clinic*, trans. A. M. Sheridan-Smith, London: Tavistock.

—— (1978) *Discipline and Punish*, trans. A. Sheridan, New York: Pantheon.

—— (1981) 'The Order of Discourse', in Robert Young (ed.) *Untying the Text: A Post-Structuralist Reader*, London: Routledge.

—— (1985) *The Use of Pleasure*, trans. R. Hurley, New York: Random House.

—— (1986) *The Care of the Self*, trans. R. Hurley, New York: Random House.

Freud, Sigmund (1919 [2003]) 'The Uncanny', in David McLintock (trans.) *The Uncanny*, London: Penguin.

Gelder, Ken, and Jane M. Jacobs (1998) *Uncanny Australia: Sacredness and Identity in a Postcolonial Nation*, Melbourne: Melbourne University Press.

Gilroy, Paul (1993) *The Black Atlantic*, London: Verso.

—— (1999) *Joined-Up Politics and Post-Colonial Melancholia*, London: ICA.

—— (2000) *Between Camps: Race, Identity and Nationalism at the End of the Colour Line*, London: Allen Lane.

Giroux, Henry A. (1994) *Disturbing Pleasures: Learning Popular Culture*, London: Routledge.

Gramsci, Antonio (1971) *Selections from the Prison Notebooks*, Q. Hoare and G. N. Smith (trans.), London: Lawrence and Wishart.

Guha, Ranajit (ed.) (1998) *A Subaltern Studies Reader: 1986–1995*, Minneapolis: University of Minnesota Press.

Hall, Stuart (1990 [1994]) 'Cultural Identity and Diaspora', in Patrick Williams and Laura Chrisman (eds) *Colonial Discourse and Post-Colonial Theory: A Reader*, London: Harvester Wheatsheaf, pp. 392–401.

—— (1996) 'When Was "The Postcolonial"? Thinking at the Limit', in I. Chambers and L. Curti (eds) *The Postcolonial Question*, London: Routledge, pp. 242–60.

—— (1997) 'Culture and Power', *Radical Philosophy* 86, 24–41.

Huntington, Samuel (1997) *The Clash of Civilizations and the Remaking of World Order*, New York: Simon and Schuster.

Jakobson, R. (1987) *Language in Literature*, K. Pomorska and S. Rudy (eds), Cambridge MA: Harvard University Press.

Kristeva, Julia (1977) *About Chinese Women*, trans. A. Barrows, London: Marion Boyars.

—— (1984) 'Women's Time', in Toril Moi (ed.) *The Kristeva Reader*, Oxford: Blackwell, pp. 188–211.

—— (1994) *Strangers to Ourselves*, trans. L. S. Roudiez, London: Harvester Wheatsheaf.

—— (2000) *Crisis of the European Subject*, trans. S. Fairfield, New York: Other Press.

Kymlicka, Will (1997) 'Liberal complacencies', accessed at http://bostonreview.net/BR22.5/kymlicka.html on 22 June 2004.

—— (2001) *Politics in the Vernacular*, Cambridge: Cambridge University Press.

Lacan, Jacques (1977a) *The Four Fundamental Concepts of Psycho-analysis*, trans. Alan Sheridan, London: Vintage.

— (1977b) *Écrits: A selection*, trans. Alan Sheridan, London: Routledge.

— (1992) *The Ethics of Psychoanalysis*, trans. Dennis Porter, London: Routledge.

Lee, A. Robert (1995) 'Introduction', in A. Robert Lee (ed.) *Other Britain, Other British: Contemporary Multicultural Fiction*, London: Pluto Press, pp. 1–3.

Lewis, Bernard (2004) *From Babel to Dragomans*, London: Weidenfeld.

Luhrmann, T. M. (1996) *The Good Parsi: The Fate of a Colonial Elite in a Postcolonial Society*, Cambridge MA: Harvard University Press.

McClintock, Anne (1995) *Imperial Leather: Race, Gender and Sexuality in the Colonial Contest*, London and New York: Routledge.

Macey, David (2000) *Frantz Fanon: a biography*, New York: Picador USA.

Memmi, Albert (1965) *The Colonizer and the Colonized*, trans. H. Greenfeld, London: Earthscan.

—— (2000) *Racism*, trans. S. Martinot, Minneapolis: Minnesota University Press.

Mercer, Kobena (1994) *Welcome to the Jungle: New Positions in Black Cultural Studies*, London: Routledge.

Moore-Gilbert, Bart, Gareth Stanton and Willy Maley (eds) (1997) *Postcolonial Criticism*, London: Longman.

Morley, David (2000) *Home Territories*, London: Routledge.

Morley, David, and Kuan-Hsing Chen (eds) (1996) *Stuart Hall: Critical Dialogues in Cultural Studies*, London: Routledge.

Morrison, Toni (1999) *Paradise*, London: Vintage.

Naipaul, V. S. (1967) *The Mimic Men*, London: André Deutsch.

Nandy, Ashis (1998) 'A New Cosmopolitanism', in Kuan-Hsing Chen (ed.) *Trajectories: Inter-Asia Cultural Studies*, London: Routledge, pp. 142–9.

Okin, Susan Moller (1997) 'Is Multiculturalism Bad for Women?', accessed at http://bostonreview.net/BR22.5/okin.html on 22 June 2004.

Parry, Benita (2004) *Postcolonial Studies: A Materialist Critique*, London: Routledge.

Phillips, Caryl (1987 [1999]) *The European Tribe*, London: Faber and Faber.

Punter, David (2000) *Postcolonial Imaginings: Fictions of a New World Order*, Edinburgh: Edinburgh University Press.

Quayson, Ato (2000) *Postcolonialism: Theory, Practice or Process?*, Cambridge: Polity Press.

Rich, Adrienne (1995) *Dark Fields of the Republic: Poems 1991–1995*, New York: W. W. Norton.

Robinson, Cedric (1993) 'The Appropriation of Frantz Fanon', *Race and Class* 35(1), 79–91.

Royle, Nicholas (2003) *The Uncanny*, Manchester: Manchester University Press.

Runnymede Trust (2000) *The Future of Multi-Ethnic Britain* (the Parekh Report), London: Profile Books.

Rushdie, Salman (1988) *The Satanic Verses*, London: Consortium Press.

—— (1992) *Imaginary Homelands*, London: Granta.

—— (1996) *The Moor's Last Sigh*, London: Vintage.

Said, Edward W. (1978 [1995]) *Orientalism: Western Conceptions of the Orient*, London: Penguin.

—— (1979) *The Question of Palestine*, New York: Random House.

—— (1981 [1997]) *Covering Islam: How the Media and the Experts Determine How We See the Rest of the World*, London: Vintage.

—— with Jean Mohr (1986) *After the Last Sky: Palestinian Lives*, London: Faber and Faber.

—— (1993) *Culture and Imperialism*, London: Vintage.

—— (1999) *Out of Place: A Memoir*, London: Granta.

Sartre, Jean-Paul (1947 [1995]) *Anti-Semite and Jew: An Exploration of the Etiology of Hate*, New York: Schocken Books.

—— (2001) *Colonialism and Neocolonialism*, (with a Preface by Robert J. C. Young, and Introduction by Azzedine Haddour; trans. by Azzedine Haddour, Steve Brewer and Terry McWilliams), London: Routledge.

Schwab, Raymond (1984) *The Oriental Renaissance: Europe's Rediscovery of India and the East 1680–1880*, trans. G. Patterson-Black and V. Reinking, New York: Columbia University Press.

Schwarz, Bill (1996) 'Conquerors of Truth: Reflections on Postcolonial Theory', in Bill Schwarz (ed.) *The Expansion of England*, London: Routledge, pp. 9–31.

Shohat, Ella (1992) 'Notes on the "Post-Colonial" ', *Social Text* 31/32, 99–113.

Slemon, Stephen (1994) 'The Scramble for Post-Colonialism', in Chris Tiffin and Alan Lawson (eds) *De-Scribing Empire: Postcolonialism and Textuality*, London: Routledge, pp. 15–32.

Smith, Zadie (2000) *White Teeth*, London: Hamish Hamilton.

Soja, Edward (1996) *Thirdspace: Journeys to Los Angeles and Other Real-and-Imagined Places*, Oxford: Blackwell.

Spivak, Gayatri Chakravorty (1987) *In Other Worlds: Essays in Cultural Politics*, London: Routledge.

—— (1990) Sarah Harasym (ed.) *The Post-Colonial Critic: Interviews, Strategies, Dialogues*, London: Routledge.

—— (1993) *Outside in the Teaching Machine*, London: Routledge.

—— (1999) *A Critique of Postcolonial Reason: Toward a History of the Vanishing Present*, Cambridge MA: Harvard University Press.

Teverson, Andrew (2003) '"The Uncanny Structure of Cultural Difference" in the Sculpture of Anish Kapoor', *Gothic Studies* 5(2) (November), 81–96.

Viswanathan, Gauri (1989) *Masks of Conquest: Literary Study and British Rule in India*, New York: Columbia University Press.

Williams, Patrick (1996) ' "No Direction Home?" – Futures for Post-Colonial Studies', *Wasafiri* 23 (Spring), 6–8.

Williams, Raymond (1983) *Keywords*, rev. edn, New York: Oxford University Press.

INDEX

DATE DUE

PRINTED IN U.S.A.

Made in the USA
Middletown, DE
17 February 2018